RESUMES

THAT MEAN

BUSINESS

RESUMES

RANDOM HOUSE

THAT MEAN
BUSINESS

DAVID R. EYLER

LIBRARY OF CONGRESS CATALOGING-IN-PUBLICATION DATA
Eyler, David R.
    Resumes that mean business / David R. Eyler.
        p.   cm.
    Includes bibliographical references
    ISBN 0-679-73120-2
    1. Resumes (Employment) I. Title.
HF5383.E95 1990   650.14—dc20   90-8306

Manufactured in the United States of America

1 2 3 4 5 6 7 8 9

First Edition

Designed by Kathryn Parise

To the divine discontent
that keeps us seeking more
—in our work and in our lives.

PREFACE

Whether you are an entry-level applicant or a mid-career executive approaching a six-figure salary, your chances of successfully applying for a new position depend largely on your power to communicate such vital information as your:

- Ability to do the job

- Appreciation for what the hiring company does

- Aspirations that are compatible with the position

- Awareness of job requirements

- Motivation to succeed

- Relevant preparation for the position

- Potential value to your new employer

All employers want assurance that you can meet these tests. Further, they want to know that you can establish this on paper clearly, succinctly, and in a convincing manner—preferably in one or two pages. That calls for top-flight resume writing skills and appreciation for what the hiring official wants to know.

Resumes that Mean Business is a highly pragmatic guide to the preparation of winning resumes. Seventy-five actual model resumes give you gut-level insights into what you should emphasize and what you should leave unsaid. Each resume is graphically critiqued to show you ideal resume length, format, and weighting of detail—what is *really* needed to bring your resume out of the stack. Example after example will show you how to convey meaningful knowledge—of what the employer *does, needs to have done,* and *why you are the person to do it.*

Supporting chapters provide you with essential information on:

- The role of your resume within the hiring process
- The employer's perspective—how your resume rates compared to others
- Your resume's role in getting you job interviews
- Word-processing, videotape, and other cutting-edge resume-preparation technology
- Job-seeking advice for individuals with special needs
- Trends in the job market

The objective is to present you with examples of a wide range of the very best resumes. All of them represent approaches to jobs from the fastest-growing employment sectors of our economy. Traditional job-seekers will glean both resume skills and useful career-potential information. Special-needs readers will gain fresh perspectives on directing successful searches with their particular purposes in mind.

David R. Eyler

Washington, DC
September, 1990

CONTENTS

INTRODUCTION

The preparation of a compelling resume is a practical art—a delicate balance of things said and left unsaid, detail provided and information meaningfully summarized, the efficient use of space and the power of pleasing graphic effect. You can learn by example and comparison. The purpose of this book is to give you the benefit of many examples and much comparison. From it emerge rules and suggestions for the right and wrong ways of composing a resume, but in the final analysis you are the judge of what makes the best case for your unique talents. The only arbiter that counts is the employer who concludes that what you have put on paper bodes well for what you will contribute to the organization's success.

Using This Book

This is a book that you will probably not read in order from cover to cover. It is arranged to let you choose the help you need and spend your time to best advantage. Still, *most* of the information will be useful to *many* people, so read this section carefully as you begin your task of building a great resume—it will guide you to the specific help you need.

75 MODEL RESUMES

The unrivaled core of this book is Chapter 3, "75 Model Resumes." Here each resume is analyzed to show you the general strategy behind the resume with 10 key points noted about the resume's content and composition. Paging through this section you will find the ideas and the inspiration to craft your own special and highly unique resume. The many examples, techniques, and formatting tips will help you pull it all together into something characteristically "you."

If you do not find your job title listed among the examples, that is no cause for concern. They were selected as a diverse group of employment categories that were both classic and contemporary—easy to extrapolate from—the kinds of situations that generalize comfortably to other fields. The professional person seeking a senior management position may well find the suggestion she needs in the example for a paraprofessional or tradesperson—and *vice versa*. You should view Chapter 3 as a repository of ideas and examples to be mixed and blended freely to your own best advantage. More details on how to do this will be presented in Chapter 1, "Preparing a Winning Resume" and Chapter 2, "How to Use the Model Resumes."

PROTOTYPE RESUMES

Three basic types of resumes serve as the prototypes for the models:

- **The Work History Resume**—sometimes referred to as a chronological resume because jobs and personal data are listed in the order they occurred;

- **The Focused Resume**—often discussed as a targeted resume because it presents capabilities and achievements in a manner that caters to a particular kind of job; and

- **The Competency Cluster Resume**—also known as a functional resume because it groups skills and qualities under headings that constitute important functions in a particular kind of job.

Chapter 2, "How to Use the Model Resumes" goes into each of these approaches to resume writing in more detail. Remember that the prototypes are offered to illustrate how you have the power to take your employment assets and, in all honesty, arrange them for their greatest impact for the situation at hand. It would not be wrong or unusual to see a successful resume incorporate the qualities of more than one prototype—or omit one or two of the prototype's expected characteristics. There is nothing exclusive or discrete in the art of resume writing—be eclectic, and comfortably use what you glean from many sources in a way that best describes you for a particular opportunity.

PRESENTING YOUR CREDENTIALS

The written resume is certainly a key element in a job search, but obviously not the only one. Chapter 4, "Cover Letters and Interviews," deals with the cover letter, the interview process, and all of the subtle things that can turn initial interest, generated by a great resume, into an offer of employment.

RESUME TECHNOLOGY

Resume writing is still basically a matter of putting words on paper in the correct and most persuasive way. Yet the influence of readily available technology is encroaching in a number of ways. Understanding it and how to use it to enhance everything from the production of your resume to your ability to prevail in the subsequent phases of the hiring cycle can mean the difference between getting the job or falling by the wayside. Chapter 5, "Computers, Fax, and Videotape," provides the advice you need to make your case most effectively.

SPECIAL SITUATIONS

If you are among those *not* making a lock-step progression to the next logical rung on a career ladder, review Chapter 6, "Special Situations." There is timely counsel for everyone in the following circumstances:

- Individuals who have lost their jobs
- Individuals returning to the organizational world after a period of family-raising or self-employment
- Students seeking part-time employment that will lead to full-time positions
- Early retirees from the military or other careers looking for new jobs
- People interested in nontraditional working arrangements that offer greater flexibility
- New citizens and foreign workers uncertain about communicating their skills in the American workplace

TRENDS

Finally, there is a closing look at the job market and the work force as it shifts to meet the realities of another century. This chapter can aid you in setting a course for a solid, successful work life. No one knows the future, but there are definite trends you should consider when planning a career. Chapter 7, "Trends in the Work Force," alerts you to what U.S. Department of Labor economists have to recommend in their most recent projections.

RESUMES
THAT MEAN
BUSINESS

1 PREPARING A WINNING RESUME

Your resume has a purpose. It must impress potential employers sufficiently to consider you further in the hiring process. It is the document that—in one or two pages—represents everything you have done to become desirable in the employment marketplace. Salary, security, and career satisfaction all depend on the job you hold. Your resume shows where you have been professionally and where you are qualified to go next.

The preparation and presentation of a resume is part of the standard job-application process. It is at once a challenge and a great opportunity to make a favorable impression. Before hands are shaken or voices heard, images and expectations are formed in the minds of those who will judge your worthiness. Your resume makes those first impressions.

Why Your Resume Is Important

The hiring official is probably considering dozens, even hundreds, of applications along with yours. Equal opportunity regulations, modern communications, and highly mobile life-styles are but a few of the most obvious factors contributing to the large number of applicants for desirable positions.

Serious contenders will know the rules of the resume game and see to it that their resumes receive serious consideration. The hiring process often begins on a negative note—reducing the number of candidates to a manageable level. Here are candidates who are not contenders:

1. The sloppy resume senders. They could be perfectly qualified or even applicants whose qualifications make them standouts in the crowd. There are often a few such people in every hiring cycle. They are fine

until someone just as good comes out of the stack who took the trouble to make a professional presentation.

2. The resistibles. Here are applicants who have dropped a stitch in the procedural quilt—they missed the "received by" date, failed to include the three references required, a college transcript, or whatever. They have given cause to be eliminated.

3. The underqualified. They lack the required master's degree or some other clearly advertised prerequisite, but thought that would be okay. Objective turndowns.

4. The negative standouts. They sent a mimeographed, unpersonalized cover letter; spilled something on their resume and sent it anyway; crossed out entries from their last try and scribbled in your key words or people; and so on. Subjective turndowns.

5. The poor communicators. Applicants who are apparently qualified, but whose resumes just don't communicate in some important regard—too much obvious fluff, too long (more than two pages, except in rare cases), sentences and paragraphs that go on and on, and so forth. They just don't come across as being capable of making their point—they are not the ones hired, if there are other choices. Largely a subjective judgment.

6. The overqualified candidates. They have held vastly superior positions or salaries, have degrees or work histories that are inconsistent with the position, etc. They fall by the wayside for inability to read the situation realistically, although they are not apt to be given that reason for the turndown. More than likely they will just find that someone else was judged to be "more appropriate" for the position.

An executive in an East Coast human resources firm wrote in a *National Business Employment Weekly* reprint (Richardson, undated):

> I keep seeing resumes that are little more than buckets into which a lot of data has been dumped in the apparent belief that I will fill in the gaps, synthesize diverse information, connect the dots, and tell you what kind of product you are. I have no incentive to do this, given the number of knights eager to enter the lists. *It is not my job to make sense out of your life.* [Italics added.]

This man reflects the plight and the attitude of many potential employers who face large stacks of resumes. It is important to recognize that you have the power to present him with what he considers material worth reading as he moves rapidly through the pile cutting it down to size.

Resume First Aid

Before we discuss the rules for writing a great resume, let's look at some examples of what can be done. Following are a series of before and after versions of actual resumes that have been improved using the recommendations in this book. Start by just comparing the visual impact of the before and after versions. Then read the point-by-point descriptions of how and why they were changed.

Phyllis J. Conners's Resume

BEFORE

General Problems

Ms. Conners's resume shows a profound lack of focus—both visually and substantively. The information is there, but she ignores the fact that resume readers will not take the time to make sense out of her life. She has to do that for them. On resumes, both the format and content must be logically presented to make the information readily understandable to readers.

Specific Points

1. If the **Objective** is going to be a simple job title, don't add qualifiers that only say the obvious—"Counselor/advisor in an academic setting" unnecessarily complicates the presentation from the outset.

2. The chronology hops and skips all over the place—if you cannot present a set of logically connecting dates, don't emphasize the irregularity by using this kind of listing. It is only recommended when one position leads neatly to the next.

3. **Experience** needs to be sorted out—as presented, the reviewer faces an interpretation task that distracts from judging overall strengths. Their job is to evaluate, not organize, your information.

4. Many of the experiences are very thin—that weakness is only made more clear by listing and describing each one separately this way.

5. With little variety in formatting, the different parts of the resume blend together. Even with just the ability to use boldface and underline, it is possible to separate the different sections.

6. **Education** is a checkoff item (you have it or you don't) for the kind of job being sought and belongs at the bottom.

7. Never offer information that might label you eccentric or different. While there is nothing at all wrong with being a dream interpretation enthusiast, it is not something to feature prominently.

8. Mention relevant skills, but play down the business aspect for this job.

9. References are obviously available upon request—no need to say so.

10. Musician information is harmless, but superfluous—she needs white space more.

BEFORE

Phyllis J. Conners
2365 Northwest Avenue, Apartment 38
Washington, DC 20017
202-912-7666

① OBJECTIVE: Counselor/advisor in an academic setting

EXPERIENCE:

1989 - Present   **Administrative Assistant: Association of Colleges Serving the Military (American Colleges and Universities), Washington, DC** Provide administrative assistance, including revising handbooks and other training materials used internationally.

② 1988 - 1989   **Conference Coordinator. American Education Association, Washington, DC** Managed logistics of national conference including: registration, travel and on-site arrangements, post-conference follow-up.

1988   **Advisor. Honors Program, The International University, Washington, DC** Advised and counseled students in large honors program; liaison between director and students; planned special cultural events.

1987 - 1988   **Counselor. Internship at The International University, Washington, DC** Led two small groups in addition to one-on-one counseling. Focus on unconscious processes as related to academic and social issues.

③

1984 - 1988   **Project Coordinator. The New Agenda, Projects JKSS, NETWORK, The International University, College of Education, Washington, DC** Managed the daily operations of an educational research office. Research duties included conducting preliminary research searches, report writing and analysis of data. Publicity duties included liaison between national media and project and dissemination of research findings. Managed logistics of training and dissemination conferences. Drafted and wordprocessed correspondence, reports and other materials. Fiscal duties included accounting, procurement and reconciliation. Supervised support staff.

1985 - 1986   **④**   **Housing Director. Shenandoah Musical Academy, Delton, VA** Administered all phases of resident housing. Duties included conflict resolution, informal counseling, supervision of student managers.

1982 - 1983   **Secretary. The International University Security Department, Washington, DC** Performed administrative personnel functions for part-time employees, including general payroll tasks, statistics, and projections. Duties included answering telephone calls, wordprocessing, typing and filing.

⑤

EDUCATION: **Master of Science in Education** (Counseling emphasis), The International University, Washington, DC, June 1988.
⑥   **Bachelor of Science in Business Administration** (Personnel), The International University, Washington, DC, June, 1983.

PUBLISHED WORKS: Three test-bank chapters in <u>Learning Theory Models</u>, Teachers Guide, Wilson & Wilson, Newhouse Press, 1987.
⑦   Articles in <u>The Finder</u>, Winter 1982, Summer and Fall 1984.
<u>Dreaming for Success</u>, Starlight Press, 1985.
"Help From Dreamers," paper presented to the Dreamers Association, Fall, 1988.

OTHER: **⑧**   Owner of Typing, Inc. - a wordprocessing business, contract researcher and wordprocessor for special projects and dissertations; contributing writer/editor for <u>The Finder</u>; freelance musician; dream counselor.

REFERENCES: **⑨**   Available upon request.   **⑩**   **⑦**

Phyllis J. Conners's Resume

AFTER

General Solutions

Ms. Conners's resume now shows unambiguously what she wants to do and lists, in order of importance, the experiences that will be of interest to the hiring official. Visually, the resume has been given several points of focus and white space separates one section from another.

Specific Points

1. The **Objective** has been simplified to communicate clearly and remove unnecessary wording that might require interpretation.

2. Since the dates of her jobs were overlapping and left gaps, they have been relegated to secondary status—provided, but not stressed.

3. Experience has been grouped in its strongest possible clusters—first that which is directly related, next the more generally related, and finally the supporting information.

4. Since the lack of primary experience in counseling will be apparent to someone in the field, the positions are related positively, but credibly, as student experiences.

5. Type size and face were changed using a computer word-processing program. Variety tends to separate the sections more clearly and gives each section greater impact.

6. Wording of her present position title was changed just enough to add an academic twist to an otherwise purely administrative job description.

7. Dream analysis is mentioned, but more matter-of-factly. The comment linking it to counseling was eliminated since the avocation may taint the professionalism of the primary field. The resume is no place to assert rights, stand on principle, or advocate special interests with any potential for raising eyebrows.

8. Word processing and research are treated more as skills, less as a business.

9. Reference availability is omitted and nothing lost.

10. Education is listed to confirm formal qualifications—no elaboration needed.

AFTER

Phyllis J. Conners
2365 Northwest Avenue, Apartment 38
Washington, DC 20017
202-912-7666

 Objective: COLLEGE COUNSELOR

 COUNSELING EXPERIENCE

- Counseling Internship: Completed a supervised practicum that was a part of my master's degree program. Consisted of leading two small groups and additional one-to-one counseling. Emphasis was on academic and social adjustment issues. The International University, Washington, DC, 1987-88.

 • Honors Program Advisor: Advised and counseled students in a large honors program. Served as liaison between students and the director. Planned cultural events. The International University, Washington, DC, 1988.

- Housing Director: Counseled students as a part of my overall duties administering a college resident housing program. Shenandoah Musical Academy, Delton, VA 1985-86.

 GENERAL HIGHER EDUCATION EXPERIENCE

- Academic Program Administrative Assistant: Provide curriculum database management for college degree programs, including revising handbooks and other training materials used in the advisement of military students internationally. Association of Colleges Serving the Military (American Colleges and Universities), Washington, DC, 1989 - present.

- Conference Coordinator: Managed the registration, travel, on-site services, and post-conference follow-up for a major national conference. American Education Association, Washington, DC, 1988-89.

- Educational Research Project Coordinator: Managed operational aspects of an educational research office, including preliminary searches, report writing, analysis of data, liaison between national media and the project, dissemination of findings, logistics of conferences, preparation of publications, fiscal management, and staff supervision. The New Agenda, Projects JKSS, NETWORK, The International University, Washington, DC, 1984-88.

- Secretary: Performed administrative personnel functions including payroll, statistics, and projections, clerical and telephone duties.

OTHER EXPERIENCE

- Writing: Authored three chapters in *Learning Theory Models*, Instructors Guide, Wilson & Wilson, Newhouse Press, 1987. Articles published in *The Finder*, 1987-88. Published *Dreaming for Success*, Starlight Press, 1985, and presented "Help From Dreamers" paper at Dreamers Association, Fall, 1988.

- Wordprocessing and Research: Owner of a private wordprocessing and contract research business.

EDUCATION

- Master of Science in Education (Counseling Emphasis), The International Univeristy, Washington, DC, June 1988.

- Bachelor of Science in Business Administration (Personnel), The International University, Washington, DC, June, 1983.

Bruce D. Ames's Resume

BEFORE

General Problems

Mr. Ames has smothered perfectly good qualifications in a sea of overstatment, misplaced emphasis, and disorganization. Adding a paragraph that gives some specifics about performance as an investment manager and deleting—or relegating to a proper place—things no one in his present career field wants to hear about his teaching days can salvage the resume.

Specific Points

1. A telephone number is essential in an age when your first contact from an interested employer is apt to be a call—he failed to list one.

2. The **Objective** leads off with rambling hyperbole that only vaguely relates to managing investments.

3. Claims of being articulate, an excellent communicator, respected leader, etc. are lost in too many words—the paragraph is actually harmful to his image and needs to be removed.

4. **Experience** is presented too broadly—there needs to be a clear division between what supports the current professional goal and that which is background.

5. Description of the investment duties is fine as far as it goes, but it lacks the performance specifics expected in such a readily quantified field.

6. The educator background is largely irrelevant to the objective of getting a better investment management position—set it apart and reduce it in size and detail.

7. Minor speeches, coaching roles, etc. have no place in this resume.

8. The securities examination is a test passed, not education gained—show it as a professional credential under the relevant job description.

9. The **Personal** information contributes nothing—delete it.

10. **Education** listings should not be vague about whether a degree has been completed or merely pursued.

BEFORE

BRUCE D. AMES

454 Hermosa Beach Drive   Los Angeles, CA 90254

OBJECTIVE

To utilize my repertoire of professional and interpersonal expertise through a dynamic position which requires exceptional communicative skills and extensive contact with the community. Special interests include investments management and marketing.

 Recognized as an action-oriented individual who possesses leadership skills and administrative ability integral to the successful implementation of projects. Welcome the challenge of working with new people and changing situations. Articulate… communicate proficiently with people at all levels. Respected for unique ability to assess needs, formulate goals and devise strategies to effectively achieve managerial objectives. Demonstrate excellent speaking, writing and research capabilities.   Capable of influencing others to perform tasks efficiently.

PROFESSIONAL EXPERIENCE

Since 1979, Assistant Vice President and Trust Investment Officer, The Bank of West Orange County. Establish investment policy, directly supervise investment administration, manage individual and comingled portfolios, evaluate accounts, securities, research and comparative performances. Monitor operations, supervise clerical functions, meet with customers and clients, represent the department.

Co-designed curriculum, taught college preparatory Math (grades 10-12) during tenure as Faculty Member at The Monument School. Developed and co-wrote <u>New Theories in Teaching Mathematics</u> and <u>Mathematics Instruction in the Private Academy</u> (1974). Directed preparation and publication of these textbooks currently used as units of instruction. Presented National 4-H Club speech (1975). As Assistant Volleyball Coach, was responsible for conditioning both boys' and girls' teams. Analyzed performance, instructed team members in game strategies and techniques to prepare for athletic competition.

At Pacific Military and Girls Academy, taught Mathematics, geometry and junior algebra. Participated in faculty and professional meetings, eduction conferences and teacher training workshops. Cultivated interpersonal skills while a Resident Adviser in a closed dormitory environment. Provided individual and group counseling services relative to problems of personal, social and scholastic nature. Assisted pupils in selecting course of study, counseled students with adjustment and academic problems. Directed dormitory orientation programs, supervised recreational and social activities.

Conducted college-level courses in Basic Mathematics and Arithmetic Theory at the Community College of the North Woods, MN, instructed prospective teachers in teaching mathematics to high school students. As Graduate Teaching Assistant at the University of Minnesota, instructed prospective teachers in Secondary Schools Teaching Methodology. Created and compiled book of formulas, presented classroom orientation lectures.

EDUCATION

Registered Securities Representative, 1979, The Bank of West Orange County.
Post-baccalaureate study (Master of Business Administration), Long Beach College, 1976-79.
Post-baccalaureate study (Master of Education Fellow), University of Minnesota, 1971-75.
Bachelor of Arts in Mathematics (emphasis, Boolian Logic Theory), University of Michigan, 1971.

PERSONAL

Strive to promote highest degree of success in fulfilling potential for self and others. Pleasures include all sports (particularly sailing, cross-country skiing, tennis and swimming) and extensive reading. Interested in developing growth-oriented programs which foster creativity in achieving objectives.

Bruce D. Ames's Resume

AFTER

General Solutions

Mr. Ames's resume has been purged of excessive words. It now defines clearly the primary and secondary information, although the format has remained essentially unchanged. A few more headings and a lot less words have transformed a weak effort into a great resume.

Specific Points

1. Telephone numbers have been added without the addition of a single line.

2. The **Objective** is now much shorter and to the point. It includes his interest in people skills and marketing, but is phrased to fit the business environment instead of a graduate school class.

3. **Experience** has been divided and reordered to place the emphasis on the business at hand—investment management.

4. A brief paragraph was added to describe his actual investment activities and performance, using a recognized standard.

5. The professional credential has been inserted at a more meaningful point.

6. Teaching is presented in the context of its current importance—proof that there was a responsible use of his time before coming to the investment world.

7. For the purposes of this resume, the teaching positions can be treated as generic events that share a common, brief description.

8. Teaching part-time while a graduate student shows some initiative, but little more relevant to the investment job; account for the periods of time and move on.

9. **Personal** was removed and left for interview small talk—if that.

10. **Education** has been clarified to list the bachelor's degree and relegate the others to their proper place as study toward degrees not completed.

AFTER

BRUCE D. AMES

454 Hermosa Beach Drive • Los Angeles, CA 90254 • 213-324-0078 (O), 213-445-0988 (R)

OBJECTIVE

 To obtain an opportunity for further growth as a Bank Trust Investment Officer, with an emphasis on marketing investment products to groups and individuals.

 ### EXPERIENCE

<u>Trust Investments</u>

1979 - Present: Assistant Vice President and Trust Investment Officer, The Bank of West Orange County.

- Establish investment policy, directly supervise investment administration, manage individual and comingled portfolios, evaluate accounts, securities, research and comparative performances. Monitor operations, supervise clerical functions, meet with customers and clients, represent the department.

- Perform as an investment generalist working with both fixed and equity funds. Use major outside contract research firm in an advisory capacity. Sit on the Trust Investment Committee. Currently responsible for the management of $150 million of personal and $276 million of institutional funds. Aggregate investment performance according to CDA has been 25th percentile nationally for the past 5 years. Regularly accompany officers from employee benefits and other divisions to assist in developing new business.

- Registered Securities Representative.

<u>Teaching</u>

Prior to beginning my investment career, I served as a teacher at two institutions:

1971 - 1973 The Monument School , Orange, CA.

1974 - 1976 Pacific Military and Girls Academy, Laguna, CA.

 In both situations, I taught Mathematics, geometry and junior algebra. Participated in faculty and professional meetings, education conferences and teacher training workshops. Cultivated interpersonal skills while a Resident Adviser in a closed dormitory environment. Provided individual and group counseling services relative to problems of personal, social and scholastic nature. Assisted pupils in selecting courses of study, counseled students with adjustment and academic problems. Directed dormitory orientation programs, supervised recreational and social activities.

 <u>Part-time Teaching During Periods of Graduate Study</u>

Conducted college-level courses in Basic Mathematics and Arithmetic Theory at the Community College of the North Woods, MN, instructed prospective teachers in teaching mathematics to high school students. As Graduate Teaching Assistant at the University of Minnesota, instructed prospective teachers in Secondary Schools Teaching Methodology. Created and compiled book of formulas, presented classroom orientation lectures.

EDUCATION
- Bachelor of Arts in Mathematics, University of Michigan, 1971.
- Additional graduate study toward the following degrees:
  Master of Business Administration, Long Beach College, 1976-79.
  Master of Education Fellow, University of Minnesota, 1971-75 (Summers).

Lan Wang's Resume

BEFORE

General Problems

Ms. Wang is a foreign student. Most of her experience and education are from China. While her resume does a good job of listing the facts of her situation, it does little to explain what she is trying to accomplish and why that is a plausible goal. Equal formatting strength is given to important and far less important items of information. The reader has to struggle to package her attributes in a way that shows her potential.

Specific Points

① Her name would be unfamiliar to most American employers—they need to know at least whether they are addressing a woman or man, if for no other reason than corresponding with her comfortably.

② None of the **Work Experience** entries describe duties, beyond job titles.

③ American and foreign experience is combined and, while not difficult to distinguish, the two should be shown more clearly.

④ **Education** lists specialized foreign certificates on a par with degrees and offers no explanation of their content or relative value.

⑤ Translation experience is useful, but the listing does nothing to enhance it.

⑥ The interpreter experience is also useful, but lacks any focus.

⑦ Office skills are worth mentioning, but need a professional context.

⑧ Typing speed is inappropriate in a resume for a professional position.

⑨ Visa status needs further elaboration.

⑩ A specific reference would be more helpful in this situation.

BEFORE

LAN WANG ①
717 Belmont Place, SE. Apartment 4122
Washington, DC 20004
(H) 202-339-1725
(W) 202-667-4612

Work Experience:

②
- **Senior Administrative Assistant, April 1989 - Present, Association of North American Colleges,** 3 Circle of the Associations, Washington, DC 20007
- **Full-Time Graduate Teaching Fellow, 1988-89** (Teaching English to foreign students - TOEFL) English Language Department, Chadwick University, CA
③
- **Instructor of English, 1982-87,** Foreign Language Department, Shenyi Teachers College, Shenyi, Linhai, China PRC
- **Instructor of English, 1987 Spring Semester,** English Training Program for Managers, Administrative Bureau of New Industry, Shenyi, Linhai, China PRC
- **Instructor of English, Grade 9, 1985 Fall Semester,** Experimental Secondary School of Linhai Province, Shenyi, Linhai, China PRC
- **Video Tape Announcer and Translator, 1982-89,** Audio-Visual Center, Shenyi Teachers College, Shenyi, Linhai, China PRC
- **Mandarin Chinese Radio Announcer, 1974-78,** Town of Mengenh, District of Shenyi, Linhai, China, PRC

Education:

④
- **M.S.- Education, Curriculum and Instruction, May 1989** (Included extensive work in TESOL and Linguistics) Grade Point Average 3.89 on 4.00 scale. Chadwick University, CA
- **Certificate, Graduate Program in English Linguistics and Literature, 1986,** Shenyi Teachers College, Shenyi, Linhai, China PRC
- **Certificate, English for College Teachers, 1983,** Dayan Institute of Technology, Dayan, Linhai, China PRC
- **B.A.- English Linguistics and Literature, 1982,** Foreign Language Department, Shenyi Teachers College, Shenyi, Linhai, China PRC

Translation Experience: ⑤

- **"Final Sayings"** - Short Story Journal of Shenyi Teachers College, January 1985.
- **History of American Literature,** Section IV, Walt Whitman.
- **Comparative Literature:** Preface to the First Edition.

Experience as an Interpreter: ⑥

- **Interpreter for Joann Williams,** Visiting English Teacher, 1985-86, Shenyi Teachers College, Shenyi, Linhai, China PRC

Membership in Professional Organizations:

- Washington Area Teachers of English as a Second Language (WATESOL)
- Association of Foreign Language Translation, PRC
- Association of International Linguistics and Literature, PRC

Office Skills: ⑦

- Experienced in IBM, Macintosh, and Apple Computers (WordPerfect, Microsoft Word, dBase, Lotus 1-2-3)
- Typing speed - 50 WPM ⑧

⑨ **Visa Status: F-1, Practical Training (9/89 - 7/90)**
Date of Birth: 7/30/56
References available upon request

⑩

Lan Wang's Resume

AFTER

General Solutions

Ms. Wang's resume has been given an introductory statement that prepares the reader for the unique combination of experiences that follows. The list of information has been broken into groups more readily grasped by the reader and brief elaborations are provided at appropriate places.

Specific Points

① The **Overview** lets the reader know that the writer is a woman, and clarifies her situation and what she is trying to accomplish. Gender would normally not be stressed, but when a foreign name does not convey enough to select a proper term for addressing the applicant, such elaboration is appropriate.

② Degrees are singled out for prominence under the **education** heading and not confused with other training which is shown later in the resume.

③ **Experience** is broken into subheadings, and listed in order of importance.

④ The most important experience is teaching in America, so it leads the list. A modest job description adds to clarity.

⑤ The Chinese teaching experience is separated from other work done there and left to stand on the strength of the job titles.

⑥ Interpreter and translator skills are combined for simplicity—similar skills.

⑦ Current position is listed as professional, but clearly not teaching. A brief statement of duties gives the position as much professional status as possible.

⑧ Office skills sound better as something related to her professional skills.

⑨ Visa status is explained enough to show an intended progression.

⑩ An approachable reference is provided to give the reader an efficient way to clarify anything at issue without getting involved in complex correspondence or awkwardly contacting the applicant before being comfortable in doing so.

After

LAN WANG

717 Belmont Place, SE. Apartment 4122
Washington, DC 20004

202-339-1725 Residence
202-667-4612 Office

 Overview: Chinese woman fluent in English, with recently completed American graduate degree, seeks opportunity to teach English as a second language to students of any language background. Also receptive to other opportunities that would capitalize on language and cultural knowledge.

Education

Master of Science - Education
Curriculum and Instruction
(TESOL/Linguistics Concentration)
Chadwick University, CA
1989

Bachelor of Arts
English Linguistics and Literature
Shenyi Teachers College
Shenyi, Linhai, China PRC
1982

Experience

TEACHING

USA

 • *Teacher of English as a Foreign Language*, English Language Institute, Chadwick University, CA, 1988-89. As a full-time graduate teaching fellow, taught English as a second language to foreign students.

CHINA

 • *Instructor of English*, Foreign Language Department, Shenyi Teachers College, China, 1982-87.
• *Instructor of English*, English Training Program for Managers, Administrative Bureau of New Industry, Shenyi, China, 1987.
• *Instructor of English*, Grade 9, Experimental Secondary School of Linhai Province, Shenyi, China, 1985.

TRANSLATION

• *Interpreter* in China for visiting American teacher of English, 1985-86.
• *Scholarly translation* of several works from English to Chinese.

OTHER PROFESSIONAL

 • *Senior Administrative Assistant*, Association of North American Colleges, Washington, DC, April 1989 - Present. Duties include assisting in the coordination of college level academic programs for members seeking college degrees throughout the world. Various roles aiding in response to user inquiries by telephone and writing. Assist in the preparation of organizational publications.
• *Video Tape Announcer/Translator*, Shenyi Teachers College, 1982-89.
• *Radio Announcer*, Mandarin Chinese language, China, 1974-78.

Related Skills

Experienced in operating IBM and Apple Macintosh personal computers.
Software proficiency: Microsoft Word, WordPerfect, dBase, and Lotus 1-2-3.

Additional Training

Certificate
Graduate Program in English Linguistics and Literature
Shenyi Teachers College
1986

Certificate
English for College Teachers
Dayan Institute of Technology
Dayan, Linhai, China
1983

Professional Affiliations

Washington Area Teachers of English as a Second Language (WATESOL)
Association of Foreign Language Translation
Association of International Linguistics and Literature

References

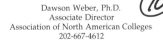

Dawson Weber, Ph.D.
Associate Director
Association of North American Colleges
202-667-4612

Immediate reference • Contact freely
• Others provided upon request.

Personal

 F-1 Student Visa currently working under the Practical Training provision.
H-1 Work Visa upon attaining permanent professional employment.
Born September 21, 1955

Do's and Don'ts of Resume Writing

There is a large body of wisdom about what you should and should not do in preparing a resume. The following is a collection of the considerations that warrant your attention. They also demand your *good judgment*—every rule does not apply to all situations and you will have to determine when to depart from the conventional approach enough to give your resume the little something extra that is appropriate in your circumstances.

Use this summary as a checklist when it comes time to plan and critique your resume.

Do	Don't
View yourself as a product to be sold to the reader of your resume.	Assume the reader has time to absorb more than the essentials.
Make your resume believable.	Stretch small or incomplete things into more than they will be if scrutinized.
Start with something that the reviewer can identify with and attach value to easily.	Bore the resume's reader.
Use only the words needed to convey your message.	Try to impress anyone with big words or philosophical statements.
Leave white space.	Fill every inch of paper with type.
Lead the reviewer through your points with headings, bullets, bold type, underlining, etc.	Get too carried away with different type faces or graphic effects that can distract instead of lead and separate.
Avoid opening up problem areas that were not required items or things clearly to your advantage.	Volunteer a photograph or similar unexpected extras—attractive, average, or too good-looking can all pose problems in the wrong situations.
Limit your resume to a page or two unless there is a compelling reason to make it more.	Use white space and formatting gimmicks to the extent that they make your resume too long.
Keep relevant content at the center of your thinking as you present your information.	Drift into listing more than the reviewer for this particular job wants to know.
Make your goals and objectives fit the job under consideration.	List your broader life goals and values in your resume.
Show that you know something about the job and the company.	Mention skills or interests that the job would never demand.
Be clear about the level of authority or responsibility for both your objective and in describing past duties.	Leave it to the reviewer to guess where you fit into the organization—theirs or the ones in your past.
Let your achievements speak for themselves—state them clearly, quantify and define where desirable.	Embellish your accomplishments—their substance has to be strong enough to convey their value.

(cont'd)

Do	**Don't**
Go easy on the adjectives.	Don't try to show action or importance with modifiers whose purpose is obvious to the reader.
Give specifics where there isn't a compelling reason not to—names and numbers let the reader judge the significance of the things you mention.	Expect the reviewer to attach importance to things that you haven't demonstrated as being significant.
Include a clear qualifications statement in your resume.	Leave it to the reviewer to figure out how your preparation might satisfy his requirement.
Use a brief summary statement that embraces your overall qualifications.	Make your summary a second resume.
Determine that the position has the potential to meet your realistic salary requirements before applying.	State a salary requirement in your resume.
Prepare a list of relevant references and make them aware of your job-hunting activity—get their permission to use their names.	List references in your resume or state the obvious—that they are available on request. Don't let an employer surprise a reference by contacting them before you do.
Resist the urge to include personal data not directly relevant to the job.	Tell the reviewer about your hobbies, number of children, excellent health, love of boating, other than professional memberships, etc.
Let your accomplishments and preparation speak for themselves.	Appraise your own worth.
List dates even in the modified resumes that are not chronological lists of past positions.	Make the dates the main feature of any resume that deserves a different focus.
Avoid qualifying statements such as "had exposure to."	Stretch your experience beyond that which can be directly claimed as yours.
State an honest reason for leaving if other than just looking for a better opportunity.	Make negative statements about the job or people you are leaving behind.
Show evidence of hard work and dedication.	Merely state that you are hard-working and dedicated—if it has to be separately claimed, you didn't communicate it substantively.
Prepare your resume professionally—that doesn't necessarily mean go out and hire someone. It does mean, at the very least, using a good typewriter and paper—try to gain access to a quality word processor.	Settle for a mechanically weak resume that looks like a something out of a beginning high school typing class.
Eliminate unnecessarily long words, sentences, and paragraphs.	Overstate your case.

(cont'd)

Do	Don't
Say enough to market fairly what you have to offer.	Be so sparse as to show disinterest or less substance than you actually have.
Proofread carefully—better yet, use a word-processing program that checks spelling, perhaps grammar too.	Commit to final copy without aging your early drafts for a few days and subjecting them to some editing.
Use a good quality paper and an interesting type style that suits your circumstances.	Choose an unusual size or color paper—same for ink, type face, etc.
Determine who should receive your resume and address it accordingly.	Send your resume to some broad entity like the personnel department unless specifically directed to do so.
Provide telephone numbers that will respond with a businesslike answer.	List a telephone number that will elicit a "she no longer works here" response, is disconnected, or otherwise fails to leave a favorable impression.
List your most recent job first.	Give the same attention to old jobs as those of recent years—condense them if necessary and make a collective statement.
List military service if it represents important employment or training—and do it in that way.	Dwell on past military experience, honors, etc. unless they relate to the job at hand.
Mention civic clubs and community service only if such activity is an expectation for the job—college president, etc.	Fill the end of the resume with a summary of everything you ever belonged to or achieved privately—Eagle Scout, pilot's license, etc.

2 HOW TO USE THE MODEL RESUMES

The resumes of Chapter 3 serve as illustrations—examples of how a resume can sell the talents of a job applicant. Their best use is as a pool of stimulating ideas, rather than as specific models to emulate with precision. To give you a framework for using this resource, the resumes have been labeled as belonging to one of three general types. In some you will clearly see the qualities of the other two—a Work History chronology may be the perfect way to end a Competency Cluster Resume, for example. The Work History Resume may be most effective if the individual job descriptions becomes miniature Focused or Competency Cluster Resumes. You are advised to see the broad potential and select the most powerful combination with which to portray your unique talents.

Resume Prototypes

THE WORK HISTORY RESUME is sometimes referred to as a Chronological Resume because jobs and personal data are listed in the order they occurred. It is the traditional resume and the one most commonly used when pursuing a regular career progression that has one position logically and continuously leading to the next.

Strengths	Weaknesses
Shows ideal job progression.	Exposes spotty career pattern.
Showcases strong employers and positions held.	Highlights inconsistencies in levels and types of employment.

(cont'd)

Strengths	Weaknesses
Sets the stage for next most logical growth move in your career.	Fails to support your aspirations if the building blocks are not there in terms of the right positions previously held. Not a career-changer's resume.
Stresses impressive job titles.	Reveals insignificant positions.
Everything easily accounted for.	Everything revealed.
Sets the stage for presenting strong references from prior positions.	Risks inviting reference checks where you would just as soon not have them.
Looks like a "real" resume—straightforward and traditional in both content and presentation.	Not particularly imaginative—relies on excellent content to give it value.
Clearly links dates of employment and verifies continuity.	Indicates breaks in employment as well as brief tenure in job.
Shows long experience.	Makes your age obvious; suggests you may have been stalled in a job too long; reveals periods of unemployment.

Work History Resume Template

> Name
> Address
> Telephone Number(s)

Overview or Summary, Goal or Objective. An appropriately brief and revelant statement of your main qualifications and goal. This is optional and can be omitted if it simply states the obvious.

Employment—A chronological list of the jobs you have held. Format can vary, but respect these rules:

- Most recent position is listed first.
- List dates continuously and consistently by month and year—or year only.
- Account for gaps in the sequence.
- Avoid showing each new position with the same employer as a new job.
  (Use a subheading approach to avoid repeating the same information.)
- State your job title.
  (Give some brief indication of what that means in the organization—the title of the person to whom you reported, for example.)
- Describe your duties and responsibilities in terms that mean something.
  (Number of people supervised and their status.)
  (Volume of business generated.)
  (Amount of change in indicators that measure what you do.)
- Mention several believable, verifiable accomplishments
  (Things that would be valued by the employers you are now seeking to impress.)
- Consolidate older and less relevant experience at the bottom of the resume.
- Respect the one-page limit—two at the most and only if justified.

Education—List your most important degree or certificate of training first in the section which, itself, will go either at the beginning or end of the resume, depending on the relative importance of your work and education. Provide name of school or college, major (if it adds to the value for the job in question), year of graduation, and state (possibly city) where college is located, depending on how well known it is.

Comments, professional affiliations, or other concluding statements can be added if kept brief and if they contribute to, rather than detract from, the main resume.

Examples of Work History Resumes

William K. Akrin
56 Tura Road
Bennington, CT 48009
203-222-9988 (Office)
203-333-9075 (Residence)

Overview

Technical Writer with formal training and experience in computer technology and technical writing seeks editorial opportunity with mass market user's magazine.

Experience

January 1985 - Present: Technical Writer
Brainware Computer Products, Inc., Bennington, CT.

Assist in the preparation of technical manuals that support the use of software products created at Brainware. Experience includes interviewing programmers and systems engineers to identify program features. Convey features and step-by-step instructions for use in lay language. Attend national workshops to receive feedback on manuals and products. Full range of mass market software including desktop publishing, graphic arts, and business packages featuring word processing, data bases, spread sheets, etc.

September 1982 - December 1985

Full-time study for bachelor's degree.

June 1980 - August 1982: Customer Service Technician
Matson Software, Ltd., Norwich, CT.

Telephone contact for users of Matson Software products including their complete line of word processing, spread sheet, graphic presentation, and data base programs. Assisted users in isolating their problems and guiding them to solutions. Maintained records on nature of questions addressed and assisted technical writing staff in the revision of manuals.

Education

Associate in Arts (AA)
Computer Studies
Asnutuck Junior College, CT, 1980

Bachelor of Technology (BT)
Technical Writing
West Connecticut College, CT, 1987

Darlene W. Robinette

96 Galveston Lane
Houston, TX 77271
713-222-9988 (Office)
713-333-9075 (Residence)

Education

Bachelor of Science   Master of Business Administration
Business Administration   Finance
Smith University, 1965   University of Texas, 1976

Chartered Financial Analyst (CFA)
1981

Experience

April 1983 - Present: **Vice President & Trust Investment Officer, National Bank & Trust of Eastern Texas, Houston, TX ($1.5 billion trust department).** Senior portfolio manager in a group of 6; managing both fixed and equity in collective and other funds (personal, pension, and endowment). Responsible for all fixed income funds (aprx $300 million personal/$100 million employee benefits); responsible for most equity funds (aprx $400 million personal/$20 million employee benefits); foundations and charities account for an additional $75 million. Involved in business development activities, including presentations to support new business and existing accounts — also cooperative development projects with other elements of the trust department. Handled installation of IBM-AT dedicated to investment function; computer literate and proficient with DOS, LOTUS, asset allocation programs, Microscan, LOTUS Financial, Norton Utilities, communications, and disk maintenance.

June 1982 - March 1983: **Vice President & Trust Investment Officer, United Bankshares Trust, Fort Worth, TX ($580 million trust department).** Chaired the investment committee. Lowered transaction costs 32 percent. Implemented standard investment procedures. Established a research capability and client newsletter. Brief tenure accrues to inability to adapt to the culture and lifestyle of the area.

July 1979 - May 1982: **Assistant Vice President and Trust Investment Officer, Chicago Retail Trust Bank, Chicago, IL ($250 million trust department).** Senior investment officer responsible for setting overall investment posture; conceived and implemented a new common trust fund, revised others. Organized and conducted investment conference for 200 members of the local professional community. Implemented formal procedures to control commission use and allocation. Established investment management goals, including performance measurement techniques. Wrote monthly economic/investment commentary for distribution to 300 regional bankers, government officials, corporate officers and selected clients.

Eight previous years: **Retail stock broker**, Scott & Delmonico, Inc., Milwuakee, WI.

Comments: Reason for leaving relates to the declining economy of the region where oil, gas, and space programs show little promise in the near future. Investment performance for the past five years: 14th percentile equities; 23rd percentile fixed income; 19th percentile combined.

THE FOCUSED RESUME is often discussed as a Targeted Resume because it presents capabilities and achievements in a manner that caters to a particular kind of job. The Focused Resume is somewhat like the Competency Cluster Resume and shares a number of its advantages and disadvantages. The emphasis in both is on extracting and highlighting selected characteristics of your work history, rather than listing it in a traditional way. The difference is that the Focused Resume aims at a particular job and is arranged in blocks of abilities and achievements, whereas the Competency Cluster Resume is more general and is centered around a series of functional areas under which your talents are grouped.

Strengths	Weaknesses
Makes a strong case for a specific type of job.	Is relatively narrow and can leave out some things that might have been valued by the reviewer.
Showcases abilities in a single light.	May have less impact than your overall experience.
Demonstrates that you know what is important to this particular employer.	You may misjudge what the emphasis should be.
Can be customized with a different focus for each of several situations.	Selectively limits your presentation.
Tends to deemphasize your employers and positions held—a strength if you are not strong in these areas.	Tends to deemphasize your employers and positions held—a weakness if it obscures outstanding entries in these categories.
Useful when you are applying for a job that does not logically flow from your last position or general work history.	Unnecessarily vague if you are building on a clear career ladder.
Useful for people with beginning or interrupted work histories—focuses on current skills, not prior jobs.	Fails to take advantage of job progression record, if it exists.
Useful where work history is scattered or has not moved at the expected pace.	Unclear for the employer who is interested in linking every statement you make to a past job.

Focused Resume Template

> Name
> Address
> Telephone Number(s)

Overview or Summary, Goal or Objective. An appropriately brief and relevant statement of your main qualifications *and goal*—the focus of your resume must be developed clearly at this point.

Abilities or Strengths or Assets.
- A series of short (a line or two) bulleted statements that tell the employer exactly *what you can do* for his company. (It requires that you know what is vital in the job.)
- Your statements reflect on your past training and experience—in the form of current abilities.
- Your statements reflect on your awareness of what the employer needs—and how you can supply it.

Achievements or Accomplishments.
- A series of short (a line or two) bulleted statements that show *what you have accomplished.*
- The more related to the job you have in mind, the better.
- Give measures of the magnitude of your achievements.
- Put them into a context that is easily evaluated by this particular employer.

Work History—List your jobs in the order held, most recent first. Dates should be given, but how you do that will depend on how much emphasis you want to place on them. Just listing the years is acceptable. If there are breaks and you want to deemphasize them, list the dates on the ragged right of the paragraph showing your employment history and make the reader look for them.

Education—List your most important degree or certificate of training first in the section which, itself, will go either at the beginning or end of the resume, depending on the relative importance of your work and education. Provide name of school or college, major (if it adds to the value for the job in question), year of graduation, and state (possibly city) where college is located, depending on how well known it is.

Comments, professional affiliations, or other concluding statements can be added if kept brief and they contribute to, rather than detract from, the main resume.

Examples of Focused Resumes

Margaret A. Arnold
89 University Drive
Santa Marina, CA 93455
805-886-1903 (Office)
805-876-3921 (Residence)

Overview

Award winning Television Support Technician with national experience in multiple aspects of professional news, talk show, and drama productions seeks network or national cable opportunity.

Professional Abilities

- SET MANAGEMENT — 6 years of experience in the management of set activities supporting news, talk show, and dramatic television productions.

- LIGHTING — 4 years as associate lighting director for a producer of nationally syndicated television musical productions. Accomplished user of Kludge and special effects lighting in television applications.

- SET DESIGN — 3 years professional and 5 years amateur set design. Professional years included assistant background construction director for the Emmy Award winning docudrama *War and Space*.

Achievements

- Union cards held in the areas of television stage management, lighting, and set design.

- On the staff of 7 production companies that received national industry recognition for excellence during my tenure.

- 1988 Audience Appreciation Award winner for set design in the live audience participation Minnie Walker Talk Show series.

Experience

June 1983 - Present: Set Manager, Gordon Boxwood Studios, Hollywood, CA.

June 1982- May 1983: Set Design Specialist, KNBB Santa Clarita, CA.

July 1979 - May 1982: Lighting Technician, Samuel Whitworth Production Company, Los Angeles, CA.

Education

Associate in Science (AS)
Electronics Technology

Allan Whetstone Junior College, CA 1979

Wadsworth T. Sandsome

35 North Island Drive
Haleiwa, HI 96740
808-675-8345 (Office)
808-776-9078 (Residence)

Position Sought

Director of Counseling Services

Abilities

- State Certified School Guidance Counselor.
- Specialized training in the recognition and treatment of adolescent substance abuse.
- In-depth familiarity with the use of computer databases designed to aid students in the selection of appropriate colleges and majors.
- Experienced group counseling leader.
- Knowledge of private as well as public sources of college bound student financial aid.
- Extensive work with private sector community work-study arrangements.

Achievements

- 80 percent of counselees admitted to college of their choice for the past five years.
- Awarded Parents' Club Award for Excellence 1989 in appreciation for efforts to establish private sector linkage between North Shore School and the burgeoning hospitality industry.
- Founder of Island Helpers Teen Substance Abuse Hotline that serves 3500 callers weekly.
- Summer Consulting Fellow to College Boardroom, a non-profit organization that designs career planning software for students.

Experience

<u>June 1987 - Present</u>: Guidance Counselor, North Shore High School, Kawela Bay, HI.

<u>June 1983 - May 1987</u>: Counselor, Kanehoe Intermediate School, Kanehoe, HI.

<u>July 1979 - May 1983</u>: History Teacher, Pearl Harbor High, Pearl City, HI.

Education

Bachelor of Science (BS)
Social Studies Education
University of Maryland, 1977

Master of Education (MEd)
Guidance and Counseling
University of Hawaii, 1983

THE COMPETENCY CLUSTER RESUME is also known as a Functional Resume because it groups skills and qualities under headings that constitute important functions in a particular kind of job. The Competency Cluster Resume is somewhat like the Focused Resume and shares a number of its advantages and disadvantages. The emphasis in both is on extracting and highlighting selected characteristics of your work history, rather than listing it in a traditional way. The difference is that the Competency Cluster Resume is more general and is centered around a series of functional areas under which your talents are grouped, whereas the Focused Resume aims at a particular job and is arranged in blocks of abilities and achievements.

Strengths	Weaknesses
Good for showing skills not apparent in recent job descriptions.	Unclear as to just which skills relate to which jobs.
Can place the emphasis on families of expertise not represented in your past work history.	Fails to support with specific sources the expertise presented.
Blurs the progress of your career in favor of concentrating on selected skills you choose to emphasize.	Represents no clear career path.
Makes the best of disjointed work experiences.	May not connect logically constructed career-building steps.
Shows a series of different skill areas.	Makes it obvious if you have only a few areas of expertise.
Can be arranged to stress current objectives rather than past history.	Lacks the support of past employment history related to current goals.
Highlights selected abilities rather than past job titles and employers.	Minimal support in the way of working experience in your current specialty.
Does not repeat similar job events.	Deemphasizes work experience.
Good for beginning or changing career directions.	May underemphasize the value of past positions held.
Able to show nonjob-related abilities such as those gained in hobbies or nonpaid employment.	You may have to explain at the interview that this experience has no base in paid employment.
An out-of-date, irregular, or irrelevant work history can be subordinated to skills you actually possess.	Expect to explain the nontraditional work history when asked.

The Competency Cluster Resume Template

> Name
> Address
> Telephone Number(s)

Overview or Summary, Goal or Objective. An appropriately brief and relevant statement of your main qualifications and goal—optional if it is obvious and adds nothing to the resume.

Competency Headings.

- Select several headings under which you can group the most valuable things you do.
- List these headings in order of importance.
- Develop under each heading a series of short statements that make it apparent that you can perform in that area of specialization.
- Use specific examples.
- Give measures of the magnitude of the skill—quantify the number of people involved, the amount of growth achieved, dollars saved, etc.
- Use names, company names, project designator, or anything that aids the reader in judging the significance of your claims.

Work History—List your jobs in the order held, most recent first. Dates should be given, but how you do that will depend on how much emphasis you want to place on them. Just listing the years is acceptable. If there are breaks and you want to deemphasize them, list the dates on the ragged right of the paragraph showing your employment history and make the reader look for them.

Education—List your most important degree or certificate of training first in this section, which will go either at the beginning or end of the resume, depending on the relative importance of your work and education. Provide name of school or college, major (if it adds to the value for the job in question), year of graduation, and state (possibly city) where college is located, depending on how well known it is.

Comments, professional affiliations, or other concluding statements can be added if kept brief and if they contribute to, rather than detract from, the main resume.

Examples of Competency Cluster Resumes

Lynn J. Andersen
973 Albacort Circle
Savannah, GA 31407
912-929-6479 (Office)
912-938-7783 (Residence)

Overview and Objective

Professional Secretary with six years of advanced office services experience
seeks Executive Secretary position with potential for assuming
an administrative management role.

Education

Associate in Science (AS)
Secretarial Science
Metropolitan Community College, GA, 1983

Professional Skills

OFFICE MANAGEMENT
- Coordination of office clerical routine.
- Schedule management.
- Vendor liaison with suppliers of services.

DOCUMENT PREPARATION
- 60 WPM using electronic typewriter or word processing equipment.
- Advanced user of principal word processing software packages.

EQUIPMENT OPERATION
- Personal computers and associated peripheral equipment.
- Fax and modems.

DICTATION/TRANSCRIPTION
- 60 WPM vocal dictation.
- Accomplished transcriber.

PERSONNEL
- Preparation and placement of advertising.
- Applicant response, appointment arrangements, EEO record keeping.

EXECUTIVE ASSISTING
- Planning of meetings and conferences, locally and at remote sites.
- Arranging business travel.
- Screening and appointment management.

Experience

<u>November 1987 - Present</u>: Secretary to the Director of Marketing, Rockaway Manufacturing Company, Ltd., Savannah, GA.

<u>May 1983 - October 1987</u>: Secretary, Jensen & Jensen Management Consultants, Tyron, GA.

Patricia D. Lyle
51-C Mount Pleasant Drive
Providence, RI 02906
401-222-9988 (Office)
401-333-9075 (Residence)

○ Competencies ○

Computer Graphics	Color and B&W graphics capabilities using Aldus Freehand on the Macintosh II computer system. Experienced in using both text and graphic scanners. Preparation of products at 300 dpi and full professional quality formats. Expert at trace modification art and logo design.
Desktop Publishing	Oversized Radius screen used for layout of single illustration and multipage publications with desktop publishing software, principally PageMaker. Experienced in brochure, tabloid, magazine, and newspaper layout — expert integration of graphics, including photography.
Drawing Board Artist	Nine years of combined college and commercial experience. Began as illustrator and paste-up person for university publications. Followed by three years of newspaper and two years of national magazine advertising and story art.

○ Awards ○

- Computer Monthly Magazine, 1989 First Place Award for Commercial Graphics
- The New England Gazette Syndicate, 1985 Award for Excellence in Advertising Graphics
- Numerous collegiate graphic arts and journalism awards

○ Employment ○

1987 - Date: Senior Graphic Artist, Rhode Island Weekends Magazine, Providence, RI

1985 - 1987: Paste-up and Insertion Technician, The Providence Daily, Providence, RI

1983 - 1985: Free-Lance Artist/Photographer

○ Education ○

Bachelor of Arts
Commercial Design
Rhode Island College of Design, 1983

○ Comments ○

Interested in taking combined artistic, journalistic, and commercial experience and applying them in a computer equipped graphic arts studio.

75 MODEL RESUMES

The resumes that follow are representative of how the standard formats can be applied effectively to a wide variety of situations. Do not be alarmed if your job title is not on the list. They are illustrations of suggested methods and styles and should not be viewed as the perfect format for a given kind of job. The job titles selected here come from the categories projected to have the best employment growth rate for this decade. Page through them all and let the cumulative impact of a lot of good ideas work for you.

While the model resumes are based on real life situations, names of people, organizations, professional terminology, numbers, and the data in general are pure fiction. They have been deliberately altered to avoid any chance of conflict with personal or proprietary information. You will be able to look at the samples and determine what real life substitutions should be made to reflect your circumstances most appropriately.

With the first two chapters as background, you should now proceed to shop your way through the rich lode of resume technique that fills the following pages. To ease your access to what might appear to be an overwhelming array of material, use the two indexes below as a starting point. The first is an alphabetical listing of all 75 resumes by job title. The second presents the same list grouped by type of resume (Competency Cluster, Focused, or Work History).

Index by Job Title

(cont'd)

#	Job Title	Resume Type	Page
4	Advertising Copy Writer	Focused	46
5	Advertising Sales Manager	Competency Cluster	48
6	Airline Pilot	Work History	50
7	Apartment Manager	Focused	52
8	Bank Collector	Focused	54
9	Bank Officer	Work History	56
10	Biological Technician	Competency Cluster	58
11	Biomedical Engineer	Focused	60
12	Bookkeeper	Competency Cluster	62
13	Business-Machine Service Representative	Work History	64
14	Chemist	Competency Cluster	66
15	Child-Care Worker	Focused	68
16	Civil Engineer	Work History	70
17	College Administrator	Work History	72
18	College Professor	Work History	74
19	Computer Operator	Focused	76
20	Computer Programmer	Work History	78
21	Computer Sales Representative	Focused	80
22	Computer Service Technician	Work History	82
23	Computer Systems Analyst	Focused	84
24	Corrections Officer	Work History	86
25	Credit Manager	Work History	88
26	Customer-Service Representative	Focused	90
27	Dental Assistant and Hygienist	Work History	92
28	Editor	Work History	94
29	Electronic Engineer	Competency Cluster	96
30	Emergency Medical Technician	Work History	98
31	Employment Counselor	Competency Cluster	100
32	Environmental Technician	Work History	102
33	Financial Analyst	Work History	104
34	Food Technologist	Focused	106
35	Fund Raiser	Focused	108
36	Graphic Designer	Competency Cluster	110
37	Heating, Air Conditioning, and Refrigeration Mechanic	Focused	112
38	Hospital Administrator	Work History	114
39	Hotel Manager	Work History	116
40	Insurance Agent	Work History	118
41	Interior Designer	Focused	120

(cont'd)

#	Job Title	Resume Type	Page
42	Landscape Architect	Work History	122
43	Legal Assistant	Competency Cluster	124
44	Library Technician	Competency Cluster	126
45	Manufacturers' Sales Representative	Competency Cluster	128
46	Medical-Records Technician	Focused	130
47	Minister	Focused	132
48	Newspaper Reporter	Competency Cluster	134
49	Nurse	Competency Cluster	136
50	Personnel Specialist	Competency Cluster	138
51	Pharmacist	Focused	140
52	Photographer	Focused	142
53	Physician Assistant	Work History	144
54	Private Investigator	Competency Cluster	146
55	Product Manager	Work History	148
56	Public Relations Specialist	Focused	150
57	Purchasing Agent	Competency Cluster	152
58	Real Estate Broker	Focused	154
59	Receptionist	Competency Cluster	156
60	Retail Buyer	Focused	158
61	Retail Salesperson	Competency Cluster	160
62	Robotic Engineer	Work History	162
63	School Administrator	Competency Cluster	164
64	School Guidance Counselor	Focused	166
65	Secretary	Competency Cluster	168
66	Securities Broker	Competency Cluster	170
67	Security Manager	Focused	172
68	Teacher Aide	Cometency Cluster	174
69	Technical Writer	Work History	176
70	Telecommunications Specialist	Competency Cluster	178
71	Television Support Technician	Focused	180
72	Training-and-Development Specialist	Work History	182
73	Travel Agent	Focused	184
74	Veterinary Technician	Competency Cluster	186
75	Word-Processing Operator	Competency Cluster	188

Index by Resume Type

#	Job Title	Resume Type	Page
3	Advertising Account Executive	Competency Cluster	44
5	Advertising Sales Manager	Competency Cluster	48
10	Biological Technician	Competency Cluster	58
12	Bookkeeper	Competency Cluster	62
14	Chemist	Competency Cluster	66
29	Electronic Engineer	Competency Cluster	96
31	Employment Counselor	Competency Cluster	100
36	Graphic Designer	Competency Cluster	110
43	Legal Assistant	Competency Cluster	124
44	Library Technician	Competency Cluster	126
45	Manufacturers' Sales Representative	Competency Cluster	128
48	Newspaper Reporter	Competency Cluster	134
49	Nurse	Competency Cluster	136
50	Personnel Specialist	Competency Cluster	138
54	Private Investigator	Competency Cluster	146
57	Purchasing Agent	Competency Cluster	152
59	Receptionist	Competency Cluster	156
61	Retail Salesperson	Competency Cluster	160
63	School Administrator	Competency Cluster	164
65	Secretary	Competency Cluster	168
66	Securities Broker	Competency Cluster	170
68	Teacher Aide	Competency Cluster	174
70	Telecommunications Specialist	Competency Cluster	178
74	Veterinary Technician	Competency Cluster	186
75	Word-Processing Operator	Competency Cluster	188
4	Advertising Copy Writer	Focused	46
7	Apartment Manager	Focused	52
8	Bank Collector	Focused	54
11	Biomedical Engineer	Focused	60
15	Child-Care Worker	Focused	68
19	Computer Operator	Focused	76
21	Computer Sales Representative	Focused	80
23	Computer Systems Analyst	Focused	84
26	Customer-Service Representative	Focused	90
34	Food Technologist	Focused	106
35	Fund Raiser	Focused	108

(cont'd)

#	Job Title	Resume Type	Page
37	Heating, Air Conditioning, and Refrigeration Mechanic	Focused	112
41	Interior Designer	Focused	120
46	Medical-Records Technician	Focused	130
47	Minister	Focused	132
51	Pharmacist	Focused	140
52	Photographer	Focused	142
56	Public Relations Specialist	Focused	150
58	Real Estate Broker	Focused	154
60	Retail Buyer	Focused	158
64	School Guidance Counselor	Focused	166
67	Security Manager	Focused	172
71	Television Support Technician	Focused	180
73	Travel Agent	Focused	184
1	Administrative Assistant	Work History	40
2	Administrative Manager	Work History	42
6	Airline Pilot	Work History	50
9	Bank Officer	Work History	56
13	Business-Machine Service Representative	Work History	64
16	Civil Engineer	Work History	70
17	College Administrator	Work History	72
18	College Professor	Work History	74
20	Computer Programmer	Work History	78
22	Computer Service Technician	Work History	82
24	Corrections Officer	Work History	86
25	Credit Manager	Work History	88
27	Dental Assistant and Hygienist	Work History	92
28	Editor	Work History	94
30	Emergency Medical Technician	Work History	98
32	Environmental Technician	Work History	102
33	Financial Analyst	Work History	104
38	Hospital Administrator	Work History	114
39	Hotel Manager	Work History	116
40	Insurance Agent	Work History	118
42	Landscape Architect	Work History	122
53	Physician Assistant	Work History	144
55	Product Manager	Work History	148
62	Robotic Engineer	Work History	162
69	Technical Writer	Work History	176
72	Training-and-Development Specialist	Work History	182

I. Administrative Assistant

WORK HISTORY RESUME

General Strategy

Ms. Williams chose the **Work History Resume** to quickly highlight her two blocks of highly relevant experience—

- four years as a military officer with leadership training, experience, and substantial responsibilities; and

- current employment in a dynamic business position that shows success in the demanding field of marketing.

A brief **Overview** section says what she has done and what she wants to do. **Comments** clarify that she wants to apply her skills assisting a senior manager with the clear implication that she views the position as a stepping stone to the executive ranks herself.

Her resume conveys the message that she has succeeded in two entry-level positions, but doesn't want to pursue either specialty as a career. Rather, she presents herself as a proven performer ready for higher-level, more general management duties. She builds her case on a foundation of clearly stated work experience that would instantly command the respect of a senior person looking for a sharp assistant who has already been in the trenches.

Specific Points

1. What she has done and what she wants to do.
2. Evidence of success in being persuasive with professional people.
3. Proven ability to communicate aggressively.
4. Industry knowledge that can be valuable assisting a senior executive.
5. Tangible proof of effectiveness in setting and meeting business objectives.
6. Relevant, applied leadership training.
7. Ability to travel and function successfully away from home.
8. Demonstrated success in taking on responsibility rapidly.
9. Tangible proof of recognition by her supervisors.
10. Relevant academic preparation for the role she seeks.

Carol J. Williams

1256 Kolorotura Drive
Washington, DC 20099
202-222-9988 (Office)
202-333-9075 (Residence)

Overview

 Strong organizational and people skills. Proven leader with over 6 years of progressively successful experience in personnel, management, and sales. Seek to combine talents at senior management level as administrative assistant with potential for assuming broader responsibilities.

Experience

June 1987 - Present: *Account Executive,* Witherspoon & Company Investments, Washington, DC. Twice awarded outstanding salesperson of the quarter as a retail stockbroker catering to professional clients. Organize and conduct on-going business development activity including extensive telephone contact and mailings. Licensed broker with broad market knowledge in a variety of industries. Generated $2.5 million dollars in new business during the last year including 8 employee benefits accounts for professional corporations.

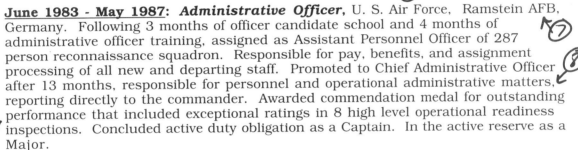

June 1983 - May 1987: *Administrative Officer,* U. S. Air Force, Ramstein AFB, Germany. Following 3 months of officer candidate school and 4 months of administrative officer training, assigned as Assistant Personnel Officer of 287 person reconnaissance squadron. Responsible for pay, benefits, and assignment processing of all new and departing staff. Promoted to Chief Administrative Officer after 13 months, responsible for personnel and operational administrative matters, reporting directly to the commander. Awarded commendation medal for outstanding performance that included exceptional ratings in 8 high level operational readiness inspections. Concluded active duty obligation as a Captain. In the active reserve as a Major.

July 1979 - May 1983: **Various part-time positions** while attending college including retail sales, secretarial positions in professional offices, and assisting my father in the operation of his consulting firm.

Education

BSc, Business Administration, Northwestern University, 1983

Comments

While I have succeeded in direct selling on the professional level, I prefer to combine that experience with my administrative talents and pursue a career in management. Combined leadership, sales, and administrative perspectives prepare me as a seasoned administrative assistant to a senior manager.

2. Administrative Manager

WORK HISTORY RESUME

General Strategy

Mr. Akrin is selling specific work experience in practical settings, not a fancy degree or a go-go career path. He selected the **Work History Resume** because he has only held two permanent positions and they showcase his greatest assets:

- He had the initiative and ability to go through all of the start-up phases of establishing a small business and saw it through to a successful operation that he sold for a profit; and

- He successfully made the transition from independent small business proprietor to manager of a reasonably complex professional office.

These two things complement each other and cast him in a good light for the kinds of employers to whom he is trying to appeal. He comes across as someone with good business sense and has demonstrated ability to fit into a traditional setting dealing with pragmatic things. This is important in his case because he has to establish that he can do more than his not-directly-relevant college degree might imply.

Specific Points

① An **Overview** is needed to say he seeks and can handle a practical administrative manager job.

② Functioned successfully in a respectable, professional setting.

③ Establishes his place clearly in the organizational pecking order.

④ Evidence of honesty in stating his level of authority.

⑤ Quantifies the level and number of people supervised.

⑥ Concise statement of what he did in the way of outside responsibilities.

⑦ Nature of the business he founded and operated.

⑧ Evidence of experience and appreciation for the business aspect of his venture—not just a clerk or artist—substantive involvement.

⑨ Shows that the business experience ended on a successful note.

⑩ Degree worth showing, but not anything to stress in this instance.

William K. Akrin
56 Tura Road
Bennington, CT 48009
203-222-9988 (Office)
203-333-9075 (Residence)

Overview

(1) Hands-on administrative manager experienced in practical business problems and solutions. Computer literate and proven successful in dealing with people: Clients, various professionals, subordinates, government officials, vendors.

Experience

(2) (3) June 1987 - Present: *Office Manager*, Johnston, Johnston, and Meeks, Attorneys at Law, Bennington, CT. Complete responsibility for the administrative operation of a 12 (4) partner general practice regional law firm. With the concurrence of senior partners, hire and supervise a staff of 9 including 4 secretaries, 2 clerks, 2 bookkeepers, and a (5) receptionist. Conduct liaison with courts, clients, and (6) vendors, including a computer consultant who maintains a Macintosh II system used in legal forms preparation, billing, word processing, and accounting.

(7) June 1983 - May 1987: *Proprietor*, The Coast Art Gallery, Delco-by-the-Sea, CT. Devised business plan, obtained (8) financing, insurance, licensing and operated a successful retail art gallery marketing the work of local artists on a consignment basis. Attained profitability in second year and (9) sold as a successful business upon relocation to Bennington.

July 1979 - May 1983: Various part-time positions while attending college including retail sales and clerical positions in two museums.

(10) Education

BA, Art History
Smith University, 1983

3. Advertising Account Executive

COMPETENCY CLUSTER RESUME

General Strategy

Mr. Kirk used the **Competency Cluster Resume** because his strong points center around two things that his potential employers care most about:

- He has managed large advertising accounts successfully and shown that he can generate new business.

- He can relate well to the creative side of the house in the advertising business because he has been there as an award-winning professional.

The college affiliation has been placed prominently because he knows his alma mater has a great reputation in the field and a lot of hiring officials are also graduates.

Work history is solid, but not exceptional. Better to lift the skills and present them as valued competencies than to try to paint a glowing picture within the context of pedestrian jobs. His **Overview** says as much—nine years of successful experience that covers both the creative and marketing sectors—strength is in making the clients happy by mustering the best efforts of his former peers in the creative part of the agency.

Specific Points

① **Overview** establishes his dual skills and identifies his industry specialty.

② **Education** is an important identity factor in his industry, so it is stressed.

③ Quantification of what he does and what it's worth in dollars is important.

④ Identifies the specific class of clients he is skilled at dealing with.

⑤ Proven ability to take over an account and make it grow.

⑥ A record for attracting new business that promises significant profits.

⑦ Shows he can bridge the gap between clients and creative people.

⑧ Experience in dealing successfully with a large, prominent client.

⑨ Major regional award from national industry group—worth mentioning.

⑩ Employment is self-descriptive to those who would evaluate him.

Hugh M. Kirk
2179 Beach Drive, Apartment 142
Jacksonville, FL
904-222-9988 (Office)
904-333-9075 (Residence)

Overview

Advertising manager with nine years of successful experience in both the creative and marketing sectors of consumer electronics. Proven ability to develop existing and new business using thorough industry knowledge and creative persuasion within the firm's specialized divisions and the client's organization.

Education

Bachelor of Science
Marketing Management
North Florida University, 1980

Account Development

Currently overseeing 6 accounts with annual agency revenues of $250,000 to $1.5 million each. Product families include consumer electronics directed toward the home-based professional and small consulting firms. Assumed management of 4 existing accounts each of which have been increased by over 20% in less than 18 months. Added two accounts in the same period, each with the potential for exceeding the annual fee volume of present largest client within 2 years.

Creative Experience

Acquired present position while serving as an independent consultant to the advertising layout department. Was employed full time to oversee the artistic development of print media advertising for the largest retail electronics chain in North Florida. Campaign won Southeast Region Style Award from the American Advertisers' Guild in 1987.

Employment Summary

Wilson & Johnson Agency, 39th Floor, Suite 300, Gulf Life Building, Jacksonville, FL. Account Executive. July 1985 to Present.

Creative Design Consultants, 15 Business Park Circle, Orlando, FL. Artistic Layout Consultant. June 1982 - July 1985.

Daytona Evening Press, 3500 Del Ray Avenue, Daytona Beach, FL. Advertising Department Apprentice. June 1980 - May 1982.

4. Advertising Copy Writer

FOCUSED RESUME

General Strategy

Ms. Baker is advised to use the **Focused Resume** because it is an efficient way to present her unique combination of talents, which would not stand out in separate job descriptions. She needs to communicate quickly to the employer—who is known to be in the business of high-fashion sportswear, since she is *focusing* on that job market—that she:

- grew up in the retail clothing business;
- has traveled to where her clients go (can identify with them as she writes copy designed to appeal to them); and
- is herself a former fashion model.

A few years as a clerk in the family store and a few more as a model turn into an attractive applicant when *focused* on the specific job she has in mind.

Specific Points

1. Brief **Objective** tells the employer she has a special combination of skills for the particular position.
2. A geographic preference is important to her, so she says so up front.
3. Worked in the industry already—with a major retailer, even though it was family.
4. Merger—a logical reason for not continuing in the family business.
5. Evidence that she knows technological as well as fashion side of sportswear.
6. Model background adds both fashion credibility and glamour.
7. Shows she has lived the lifestyle of those for whom she intends to write.
8. A highly respected agency, known in the region, endorses her stature.
9. Advantage to being in the family—saw all sides—more than a clerk.
10. Respectable liberal arts degree is fine for what she is trying to achieve.

Kathryn C. Baker

38 Ohio Place, Apartment 403
Rapid City, SD 57709
605-222-9988

① **Objective:** Copy writing position in an established mail order firm in the
North Central region. Particularly interested in applying strong sense of
② style and knowledge of top market sportswear gained working in family
retail clothing business and modeling career.

ASSETS

③ • **Overall perspective** on the national sports clothing market from a
lifetime of participation in my family's store which was the 2nd largest
retailer of sportswear in Minnesota prior to its acquisition by a national **④**
chain upon by father's retirement.
⑤ • **Familiarity with the trends and technological features** associated
with contemporary all-weather sports clothing.
• **Fashion sensitivity** in the sports garment industry enhanced by over 2
⑥ years of successful modeling in Chicago market following college
graduation.
• **Extensive travel** throughout the winter sports areas of the United
States, Canada, and Europe. **⑦**

EMPLOYMENT

⑧ **The Wood Agency**, 1000 Market Square, Mercantile Center, Chicago, IL.
Model specializing in active sportswear. June 1987 - January 1990.

⑨ **Outdoor Classic Design**, Wilmount Mall, Minneapolis, MN. Seasonal
sales work in family business from age 16 through college. Observed and
participated in buying and merchandising as well.
December 1978 - June 1987.

⑩ ## EDUCATION

Bachelor of Arts
Liberal Arts
National College, 1987

5. Advertising Sales Manager

COMPETENCY CLUSTER RESUME

General Strategy

Mr. Kearney decided to bracket his employment so boldly that it needed no heading, such as Objective. In six words he makes clear:

- what he wants to do—sell radio advertising;

- the level at which he wants to operate—management; and

- the market for his talents—top-ten radio.

With that taken care of, the best way to proceed is with the **Competency Cluster Resume** where he continues the powerfully simple message he has begun. The headings alone say he is competent in marketing, management, creative, and technical aspects of his specialty. He then goes on to say exactly how under each heading, briefly puts forth a career path that endorses his readiness for sales management, and concludes with a pair of degrees that complement what he is trying to do occupationally.

Specific Points

1. Six introductory words can say a lot about what you want to do.

2. Sidebar headings themselves serve as an outline of competencies.

3. Identifies the specific market niche in which he is knowledgeable.

4. Quantifies sales productivity with dollar figures and percentage of growth.

5. Shows he can develop other salespersons—a key skill for a sales manager.

6. Proves he is a creative ad man—major station/regional awards/ bonuses which are only paid when efforts generate the profits to pay for them.

7. Demonstrates early work ethic and shows valuable experience as a DJ.

8. Even a simple electric typewriter will generally **bold** and <u>underline,</u> adding interest to the resume and distinguishing between levels of headings.

9. Career path is shown clearly in this simple listing of positions held.

10. Degrees listed vouch for general education and specific business preparation relevant to a career in sales management.

Alfred D. Kearney
289 Atlantic Boulevard
Alameda, CA 94502
415-722-9988 (Office)
415-443-9075 (Residence)

① **Advertising Sales Manager, Top-Ten Radio**

② **Marketing**

③ Successful radio advertising sales experience for major market top-ten station. Established in the college and young adult market segments including physical conditioning, fast food, and sportswear. Servicing 37 ④ accounts with annual ad budgets in the $4000 to $175,000 range yielding combined yearly revenues of $3.2 million. Increased account dollar value base by average of 30% annually while adding new accounts at a rate of 2 monthly.

Management

⑤ Developed a team of six junior sales representatives from point of recruitment through field training and into independent operation. Retained 4 of the 6 after 2 years with 2 earning individual productivity awards and all substantially exceeding minimum production objectives.

Creative

⑥ Three years as advertising copywriter for lead station in the Western Radio Group. Twice earned regional awards for creative impact and client retention. Each involved substantial, documented, renewal bonus.

Technical

⑦ During 4 years of college, worked average of 20 hours weekly as combination disk jockey and station engineer for mid-size university town AM station serving a comprehensive rural market.

⑧ Employment

WQRA Alameda, Group Advertising Sales Manager. 1983-Present.

⑨ WLUX Phoenix, Advertising Copywriter. 1980-83.

WTBP Manhattan, KS, Disk jockey/engineer. 1978-83.

Education

Associate in Science ⑩ Bachelor of Science
General Studies Business Administration
West Kansas Junior College, 1978 Manhattan College, 1983

6. Airline Pilot

WORK HISTORY RESUME

General Strategy

Ms. Johnson is following a defined career path in an industry that has specific building blocks of experience—perfectly suited to the **Work History Resume** in which everything can be shown in the expected order:

- small aircraft charter pilot;

- lowest cockpit officer, but in a commercial freight aircraft;

- command experience in a reasonably complex passenger aircraft; and

- her current aspiration to enter the major carrier field as a second officer.

In such well-defined situations, not a lot has to be said in the resume since much of the wording is "code" that says volumes to those specialized hiring officials who will read it. You don't have to tell someone in such a role what it means to command a Dash-7; they already know the magnitude of such experience. The same would be true of other specialty occupations—flying just happens to be the example used in this resume.

Specific Points

1. A clean, modern type style is available on many computers—it is a suitable choice for technical resumes and adds interest.

2. Though cryptic, the **Objective** instantly states her aspirations in language readily understandable within her industry.

3. Evidence that she has logged the requisite hours at this level of experience.

4. Opportunity to show that she has experienced severe-weather flying.

5. Demonstrated ability to deal with mechanical in-flight emergency.

6. Has already experienced the large commercial aircraft environment.

7. Served time at the entry level and dealt with passengers directly.

8. Has the right degree for a commercial flying career.

9. Shares alumni status with people in the industry—well-known college.

10. Certifications highly relevant in this line of employment.

Mary E. Johnson
8356 Madison Street
Grayslake, IL 60030
312-612-9988 (Office)
312-343-9075 (Residence)

Objective

Second Officer•Passenger Jet Equipment•National Airline

Experience

October 1986-Present. **Captain, Flying Commuter Air**, Chicago, IL. After serving 1 year as Second Officer, first in Beach 99, then Dash 7 aircraft, advanced to Captain in the latter. Have logged 34,398 hours total flying time, 7312 as Captain. Experience in all-weather conditions of the upper Midwest. Commendation for successful handling of in-flight emergency relating to complete power loss in number two engine on final.

August 1984-September 1986. **Flight Engineer, Corporate Charter, Inc.,** Orlando, FL. Served as Third Officer on four engine turbojet air freight cargo equipment operating nightly between Central Florida and Memphis.

June 1980-July 1984. **Charter Pilot, Wilson & Davis Aviation**, Pensacola, FL. Flew individuals on daylight sightseeing, photographic, and point-to-point business trips using single-engine Cessna 180 and similar aircraft.

Education

Bachelor of Science
Aeronautical Engineering
Embry-Riddle Aeronautical University, 1980

Professional Certification

FAA Certified Commercial Pilot, Multi-Engine, Instrument Rated

7. Apartment Manager

FOCUSED RESUME

General Strategy

Mr. Blakemore is making application within a specialized employment field and is advised to use the **Focused Resume** in order to:

- highlight his professional certification and minimize his lack of a college degree, which is not overly relevant here and easily compensated for; and

- stress the base of successful experience doing exactly what he is asking to do in yet a larger, higher-paying facility.

This resume format is ideal for placing the emphasis on the skills, experience, and training most immediately applicable to the position in question.

Specific Points

① **Overview** is used to categorize immediately the scope of his experience.

② It is also the place to establish the existence of his instantly credible professional certification, the Certified Building Manager (CBM) designation.

③ Tells what kinds of projects he has managed and for how long.

④ Says what the employer wants to hear—occupancy up, turnover down.

⑤ Can supervise the sort of employees known to exist in the new setting.

⑥ Experienced in dealing with a union work force.

⑦ Gets along well with the project staff—an essential quality for a manager.

⑧ Knows how to deal with tenant organizations.

⑨ Work history shows responsible positions logically supporting aspirations.

⑩ Has at least some formal business training.

Wilson W. Blakemore

3179 Clayton Place, NW
Washington, DC 20039
202-821-9988 (Office)
202-538-9075 (Residence)

Overview

Residential property manager with 16 years of progressively more responsible positions in 250 to 500 unit up-scale apartment projects. Certified Building Manager (CBM) with highly successful combined operating and marketing experience.

Strengths

• **Managed 2 general population buildings**, each for a period of approximately six years prior to assuming general management of present major senior retirement complex in 1985. Occupancy increased from mid-70% to 95% range in each situation with corresponding reductions in tenant turnover.

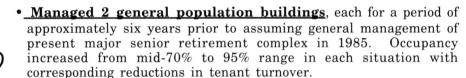

• **Oversaw building engineers, building and grounds maintenance staffs, contract marketing efforts, and lobby personnel** in each facility. Twice in collective bargaining situations. Staff retention raised from average of 8.3 months to over 3 years in high attrition positions. Executive staff stabilized completely.

• **Successfully dealt with tenant organizations** in each situation. Established sufficient goodwill to reduce litigation to management companies involved by an average of 30% within 1 year of assuming duties. Led crucial tenant relations campaign resulting in voluntary condominium conversion of major inner city property following 8 years of costly opposition.

Employment

• Simonton Place Apartments, 487 unit seniors' rental facility, predominantly 2-bedroom, top-decile rent category. Washington, DC, General Manager. 1985-Present.

• Wilkins Gardens, 364 unit general population rental complex, mixed 1, 2-bedroom, and efficiency building with extensive grounds including golf course. Richmond, VA. Resident Manager. 1979-1985.

• Randal Place Apartments, 295 unit young professional building, 85% efficiencies, remainder 1 and 2-bedroom, mid-town location. Washington, DC. Resident Manager. 1973-1979.

Education

Diploma
Business Management
District Business College, 1983

8. Bank Collector

FOCUSED RESUME

General Strategy

Mr. Rogers has completed a career in the navy with an outstanding record and a lot of highly relevant skills. He needs to showcase those talents without drawing undue attention to the fact that they were gained while working in a military environment and for a single employer. His best approach is to use the **Focused Resume,** with which he can establish that he:

- welcomes the challenge of public contact and problem solving;

- has comparable skills to someone in a personnel career in the civilian sector;

- has been successful in positions of considerable responsibility; and

- possesses the practical training necessary to do the job.

Specific Points

(1) An **Objective** statement makes it clear that he is willing to take on the challenge of solving problems with the general public—a general focus suited to many civilian jobs, including Bank Collector.

(2) Immediate verification of his experience in dealing with people.

(3) Qualification of the scope of his responsibilities and the fact that they dealt with financial matters.

(4) Notes that current technology was available to him in his environment.

(5) Experience in relating to all levels of clients—junior to very senior.

(6) Was an innovator in using the same kinds of technology called for in a bank conducting credit collection efforts over a large region.

(7) Verifiable success in handling sensitive issues to the satisfaction of the customer would be attractive to those reading his resume.

(8) Another specific illustration of initiative and successful results.

(9) A simple statement of work history that speaks for itself.

(10) A brief **Comments** statement can do a lot to meld experience with objective—bridges the gap between careers in divergent settings.

Charles L. Rogers
9075 Salem Place South
Augusta, GA 30901
404-662-9988

 Objective: To obtain a business position that involves problem solving and public contact.

Strengths:

 • Twenty year career as a Navy non-commissioned officer in the personnel specialty — customer service and problem solving.

 • Managed a 9 person office adjudicating pay and benefits claims for a command (customer base) of 7,000 sailors.

 • Conversant in telemarketing techniques and equipment as applied to financial applications.

• Mature, experienced manager accustomed to dealing successfully with diverse clients ranging from new enlistees to senior flag officers.

Achievements:

 • Established an 800 number service line for Navy pay and personnel problem resolution.

 • Increased customer satisfaction rate by 42 percent while reducing staffing and support costs by one-half.

• Set record for Navy Fund (United Way-type organization) participation in the Pacific Command by using telephone solicitation techniques.

Work Experience:

1969-1989: United States Navy

Education:

Diploma
Office Management
Wilson Business School, 1969

Comments: Enlisted in the Navy following graduation from business school. During 20 years of service, attended an on-going series of professional development courses in the personnel and financial services specialties. While work experience has been limited to military, human relations and financial skills are essentially the same as among civilian clientele.

9. Bank Officer

WORK HISTORY RESUME

General Strategy

Ms. Anson chose the **Work History Resume** because she has a straightforward pattern of employment in her professional field. It is effectively described by listing each position in order and detailing her various responsibilities:

- starting with minor experience in the industry as a summer teller;

- beginning her professional lending career in the recognized entry-level position of credit analyst; and

- moving up to Assistant Loan Officer.

Her well-ordered, brief resume establishes that she is moving successfully through the progression expected for the next step in her career ladder—a lateral move to a better opportunity or larger institution or a promotion to full fledged Loan Officer status.

Specific Points

① The **Overview** effectively states level of experience in a single sentence.

② Continuity is shown by the dates of employment at each institution.

③ Large employers like these are understood in their industry—no further description of them is necessary.

④ The position title is sufficient to tell those in the business the kind of work she does—what is needed is enough quantification to describe exactly what level of responsibility she had in the position.

⑤ When it can be safely verified by future reference checks, ranked performance is a strong way to demonstrate strength.

⑥ Expected background experience is established by this entry-level position.

⑦ Shows rapid, successful assumption of responsibility.

⑧ Discreet, matter-of-fact explanation of reason for leaving first position.

⑨ Career-oriented degree shows commitment to the profession.

⑩ Professional affiliations are enhanced by noting a leadership role.

Sally N. Anson
8567 South Murray Lane
Columbia, SC 29205
803-222-9988 (Office)
803-333-9075 (Residence)

OVERVIEW

① Commercial lender with four years of successful experience
in regional bank lending to middle market accounts as a credit analyst
and corporate calling officer.

EXPERIENCE ③

② **June 1987 - Present**: *Assistant Loan Officer,* **Southland Banks**,
Columbia, SC.   Commercial loan officer with extensive business
development responsibilities in the Carolinas, Georgia, and North Florida.
Manage a $35 million portfolio which includes $27 million outstanding and
$8 million committed. Generated $11 million in new deposits and $19
million in new loans in 2.5 years — number 2 performer on a staff of 12 ⑤
regional lenders.

④ ⑥
June 1985 - May 1987: *Credit Analyst,* **Coastal National Bank**, Sea
Pines, GA. Entry position upon college graduation. Credit review and
analysis for middle market companies. Rapidly assumed full supporting
activities for lenders prior to leaving and assuming an officer position in ⑦
the interest of professional growth not available at Coastal National. ⑧

July 1981 - May 1985: Various part-time positions while attending college
including seasonal retail sales, clerical positions and **summer
employment as a bank teller**.

EDUCATION

⑨→ Bachelor of Business Administration
Banking and Finance
University of West Georgia, 1985

⑩ ## PROFESSIONAL AFFILIATIONS & TRAINING

Professional Member, Robert Morris Associates,
Secretary of Carolinas' Chapter.
Currently pursuing the National Commercial Loan School,
Norman, Oklahoma.

10. Biological Technician

COMPETENCY CLUSTER RESUME

General Strategy

Mr. Woodward is just completing his college studies and, while he has some valuable experiences, they do not lend themselves to a traditional resume where dates must show continuity, one position follows another, etc. Because his experience is part-time and irregular, but important to potential employers, he was advised to use the **Competency Cluster Resume.** This allows him to say precisely what he did—and even where and when he did it—but without having to emphasize the mixed nature of his experiences.

With this approach, he can clearly highlight the fact that he:

- has laboratory work experience;

- has field experience;

- has contributed to formal research; and

- was educated for this speciality.

Specific Points

① Combined and categorized, two summer jobs take on greater meaning.

② Work ethic demonstrated by evening employment during college.

③ Classifying his and his supervisor's levels of responsibility defines the magnitude of the work done.

④ Field experience for a regionally known organization is worth noting.

⑤ Establishes a lifelong working knowledge of applied animal biology.

⑥ Cites applications that will be valued by the kinds of firms apt to hire him.

⑦ Associates himself in an appropriately limited way with known research.

⑧ The right degree for his career, earned from a respected local institution.

⑨ Notes a nationally recognized association's accreditation of his program.

⑩ An entry-level person, in particular, needs strong, relevant references.

Vernon D. Woodward

1279 Creek Valley Avenue
Pittsburgh, PA 15214
412-222-9988 (Office)
412-333-9075 (Residence)

LABORATORY EXPERIENCE

 • Two summers of full-time experience assisting biochemists at University Associates, Inc. in the analysis of test-animal body fluids, drug reactions, and food assimilation studies.

 • Evening employment with National Labs in the capacity of a biological technician aide during final academic year. Assisted senior microbiological technician in immunological research.

FIELD EXPERIENCE

• Summer experience with Save The Lake Foundation assisting wildlife biologists in the collection of data on the effects of pollution on the ecosystems of Western Maryland.

 • Grew up working on family poultry farm constantly involved in practical application of nutrition and disease management including assisting in taking blood samples, mass vaccination drives, on-site analysis and data gathering by feed contractor's scientists.

RESEARCH CONTRIBUTIONS

• Acknowledged for supporting efforts in Wilson-Walker study of immunological parasitology in farm/college environments, 1987.

EDUCATION

Associate in Applied Science
Laboratory Technology
Allegheny Junior College, 1989

COMMENTS

Formal clinical training in AJC's nationally accredited program in Laboratory Technology supplemented by significant periods of employment in the industry on a part-time basis. Life-long exposure to applied application of laboratory technology in field settings. High motivation and competency verifiable by references upon request.

11. Biomedical Engineer

FOCUSED RESUME

General Strategy

Ms. McNair has excellent credentials, but a history of short terms of employment. Her choice of the **Focused Resume** is a wise one because it tends to showcase her strong abilities and achievements without making the employer search for them in a string of positions that didn't last very long. All of her employers are important names to mention and the dates are not withheld, just not emphasized.

With this approach, the reviewer's attention is *focused* on:

- six powerful sets of professional skills;
- three clearly important professional achievements;
- six nationally recognized employers; and
- the right degrees and affilations.

Specific Points

(1) A headline-type **Objective** classifies the field and level of employment.

(2) Established abilities in the technical specialty.

(3) Indications of ability to lead other scientists and work within standards.

(4) Proof of being able not only to design, but to implement her achievements.

(5) Security clearances may be an attractive asset worth mentioning discreetly.

(6) National professional recognition establishes stature in her field.

(7) By moving the dates of employment to the right of the employer and not making them a separate column, they are deemphasized, but available.

(8) Rapid movement to more important job titles does much to compensate for relatively brief tenure with various employers.

(9) Excellent degrees and universities discreetly noted.

(10) The expected professional affiliations are confirmed.

Edith K. McNair
8236 Thurmont Street
Petersburg, VA 23805
804-333-9075 (Residence)

① OBJECTIVE: Biomedical Engineer — Research and Development

ABILITIES:

② • Apply computer aided design to advanced prosthesis testing
• Adapt artificial intelligence to mechanical applications
• Direct design staff integrating digital/mechanical dimensions
③ • Liaison with civilian and military government scientists
• Conduct feasibility testing within established industry standards
• Coordinate with regulatory boards on operating approvals

ACHIEVEMENTS:

④ • Designed and implemented advanced aerospace prosthesis applications for
    unmanned environments
• Applied CAD/CAM principles to previously unapproached design areas within the
    aeromedical arena (details classified) ⑤
• Woman Engineer of the Year Award winner in 1987 for work in articulating joint
⑥   modification mechanics in AI theory

WORK HISTORY:

• Woodruff Laboratories, 1988-89   Senior Scientist
• Digital Medical Corporation, 1985-88   Applications Developer
• Johnston Medical, Inc., 1984-85   Design Engineer
• NASA, 1982-84   ⑦   Biomedical Researcher   ⑧
• Johns Hopkins University, 1980-82   Graduate Assistant
• United States Air Force, 1976-80   Engineering Instructor

EDUCATION:

Bachelor of Science   ⑨   Master of Science
Mechanical Engineering   Biomedical Engineering
Virginia Polytechnic Institute, 1976   Johns Hopkins University, 1982

PROFESSIONAL AFFILIATIONS:

• Society of Women Engineers
• Biomedical Engineering Society
⑩

12. Bookkeeper

COMPETENCY CLUSTER RESUME

General Strategy

Mr. Joseph has only held one position, but he has the kinds of abilities that would be very attractive to an accounting firm looking for a bookkeeping associate. The best way to display his strengths is with the **Competency Cluster Resume.** It allows him to relegate his single employer to the bottom of the page and draw attention to his most marketable qualities:

- an associate degree in accounting from a respectable local college;

- experience preparing taxes for small business clients;

- outstanding applied knowledge of accounting-related computer software; and

- a willingness and ability to work directly with clients.

Specific Points

1. In the absence of a long work history, the academic credential is important.

2. Practical, quantified experience with which the employer can identify.

3. Bread-and-butter business for the kind of firm he seeks to join.

4. Demonstrates software knowledge and proper role relative to professional staff—knows how to fit into the team.

5. Ability to use an important class of software and an indication that he can figure out the use of others by using the manuals provided.

6. Knowledge of relevant computer hardware and peripheral equipment.

7. Valuable skills in using computer communications equipment and programs are alluded to in this point.

8. Level of responsibility indicated by representing the firm to clients directly.

9. Respect for professional strengths and limitations shown here—i.e., won't be getting the firm into trouble by making decisions better left to the CPAs.

10. Solid, continuous employment history with an established firm.

Enrique E. Joseph

491 Baldwin Place, Apartment 29
Corpus Christi, TX 78404
512-261-9988 (Office)
512-443-9075 (Residence)

Education

 Associate in Science
Accounting
Bee County Junior College, 1986

SMALL BUSINESS TAXES

 • Maintain ledgers, statements, and running status forms for 36 small business clients.

• Prepare federal and state quarterly withholding forms for clients.

COMPUTER USE

• Enter tax data into TaxWise software under the direction of professional staff of CPA firm.

• Data entry and routine analyses using the Primary Spreadsheet software package and related manuals.

• Data entry and reports generation using the Twin Ledger II system on the ProCal 37 computer and operating system.

• Operate modem data exchanges quarterly with 3 large client companies.

CLIENT CONTACT

• Serve as point of contact for 17 small business owners whose books are maintained by the firm.

• Explain reporting procedures and respond to client assistance requests not involving CPA advisories.

Employment

1986 - Present: Bookkeeper
Bell & Weathers, CPAs, PC

13. Business-Machine Service Representative

WORK HISTORY RESUME

General Strategy

Ms. DuVall has held two positions that display her talents quite well. For that reason, she has chosen the **Work History Resume** format. It allows her to show:

- the right kind of formal technical education;
- inside technical service employment;
- field service employment; and
- an impressive array of manufacturers' specialized training schools.

Specific Points

(1) The applied electronics degree is a valuable asset worth using as a lead item in this resume directed toward technical employment.

(2) Current employment is both verified and described as relevant.

(3) Position title is self-descriptive, but needs further qualification as to whether she was a generalist serving many lines or a specialist limited to one or two categories of equipment.

(4) Competency as confirmed by a competitive award is worthy of mention.

(5) Customer relations is very important in this field and her ability to cite strength in that area adds value to her credentials.

(6) Demonstrated in-house competence speaks well for her ability to coordinate field troubleshooting with the main office staff—speaks their language—has "been there."

(7) Good to specify the kinds of service work done—warranty, preventive maintenance, etc.

(8) Current manufacturer-specific training is invaluable—stress it if you have it.

(9) A subtle expression of willingness to travel and pursue opportunities for technical growth is also conveyed in this list of courses attended.

(10) Progress in achieving formal professional certification should be noted.

Elaine P. DuVall

472 Ross Road, NE
Frederick, MD 21702
301-222-9988 (Office)
301-333-9075 (Residence)

Education

① Associate in Applied Science
Electronics Technology
Middletown Community College, 1983

Experience

June 1987 - Present: ② ③ Technical Representative, Micro Copiers & Office Electronics, Inc., Frederick, MD. Install and service complete line of office copiers, mail processing, and ④ personal computer equipment on site. Runner-up in Mid-Atlantic Region Xeno Technical Trouble Shooting Contest last year. Customer satisfaction bonus this year. ⑤

June 1983 - May 1987:

major

⑥ Bench Technician, Wilmont Office Systems, Rockville, MD. In-house service technician responsible for repairs to all kinds of office electronics products. Testing, preventive maintenance, and component ⑦ replacement on top lines under warranty of manufacturers. Formally recognized for outstanding performance on six occasions.

⑧ Specialized Manufacturers' Training

• October 1983 — 2 week resident course, Xeno Corporation Training Center, Portside, NC, Copier Repair Courses I & II.

• April 1984 — 1 week resident course, Mika Computers Technical Center, Palo Alto, CA, Office Computer Trouble Shooting Basics.

⑨ • July 1986 — 10 day seminar, Appricot Service Center, Taos, NM, Upgrading and Maintaining Appricot Computer Systems.

• September 1987 — date: Computer Assisted Instruction courses by the Office Electronics Institute in preparation for certification tests. Passed Series I & II, completion of Series III & IV anticipated in 1989 for designation as a Certified Office Electronics Technician (COET). ⑩

14. Chemist

COMPETENCY CLUSTER RESUME

General Strategy

Dr. Hasenworth has outstanding credentials, but her experience does not include full-time employment outside the academic community and related work-study positions. She is advised to stress her excellent abilities and all that she has achieved, without drawing undue attention to the fact that she has never held a job. The **Competency Cluster Resume** is the best format for accomplishing this. With it she can show that she:

- knows where her training can best be used in industry;

- has the industry-related skills and achievements to be attractive; and

- holds academic credentials appropriate to an advanced research position.

Specific Points

1. In a brief introductory **Objective** sentence, she establishes that she is pursuing a position in industry, not the academic world.

2. Practical, industry-related research is noted vs. the esoteric, academic variety that might be of less importance to the people who will read her resume.

3. Computer literacy appropriate to her field is established authoritatively.

4. Sensitivity to a possible role as an industry spokesperson to environmental and other community groups may make her a more attractive candidate in today's climate, which is filled with such concerns.

5. Linkage with a respected industry group as credibility by association.

6. Evidence of working with up-to-the-minute issues and technology.

7. National stature confirmed by competitive award in her field.

8. Respect of mentors implied by selection for key studies and publications.

9. The correct academic credentials are in place for top-level research.

10. References are key to confirming her qualities and potential in the absence of a traditional employment record.

Jill C. Hasenworth

367 Jamesway Avenue
Overland Park, KS 66211
913-333-9075 (Residence)

 OBJECTIVE: An advanced research position within the polymer coatings segment of the paint industry.

COMPETENCIES:

 • Designed polymer coating testing procedures based on computer modeling and mathematical weather effects simulation.
• Extensive computer programming capabilities in specialized scientific languages and servo linkages among non-complementary systems.
• Outstanding lay communication skills invaluable asset in articulation of scientific needs and achievements to broader scientific and business constituencies.
• Broad industry exposure across the specialized polymer segment gained during work-study and research fellowships supported by the Polymer Council over five years of graduate work-study.

ACHIEVEMENTS:

• Applied attrition analysis assumptions successfully to the oblique abrasion theory permitting breakthrough advances in space age coating durabilities.
• Placed second in national competition sponsored by American Chemical Institute's Polymers Division in new research articulation.
• Selected as one of a team of three doctoral students to continue the grant-based work of Hans Bremmer in polymer isolation.
• Dissertation entitled "Assumptive Bremmerian Polymer Attitudes Beta Testing" published as a monograph of the ACI Institute, Polymers Division.

EDUCATION

Doctor of Philosophy
Theoretical Polymer Chemistry
University of Chicago, 1989

Master of Science
Chemistry
University of Chicago, 1985

Bachelor of Science
Chemistry
Ottawa University, 1983

COMMENTS

Extensive work-study experience in a variety of industry settings adds practical dimensions to my theoretical training. Upon request, references will be provided to substantiate my performance in those settings.

15. Child-Care Worker

FOCUSED RESUME

General Strategy

Ms. Busch has a specific goal in mind that calls for presenting a rather specific set of strengths—she can do this most effectively by using the **Focused Resume** since it makes these qualities the central focus of her presentation. With it she is able to:

- show that she is formally trained for the position she seeks;

- qualify the level of position and the setting she most values;

- enumerate her five greatest strengths unencumbered by spreading them across a series of different positions;

- properly establish work experience; and

- verify important certification and affiliation.

Specific Points

1. Legitimacy and professionalism are conveyed by her formal training at a known institution.

2. Precisely what she seeks is noted up front—including private-sector setting that will make clear her commitment to business day-care.

3. Institutional experience separates her from home child-care applicants.

4. Directly addresses community concern with health and character.

5. Demonstrates familiarity with child-care in a variety of settings.

6. References alluded to—essential in such a sensitive position.

7. Work history is brief, but establishes context for strengths noted above it.

8. Verification of required licensure.

9. Certification of personal health and character available.

10. Member of national association that espouses professionalism and high standards.

Lois M. Busch
672 Pocatello Drive, Apartment 78
Lewiston, ID 83501
208-333-9075 (Residence)

EDUCATION
(1)
Certificate
Child-Care
Boise Community College, 1983

POSITION DESIRED
(2)
Child Care Director — Private Sector

STRENGTHS

- Six years of progressively more responsible experience as a child care paraprofessional in institutional settings. (3)

(4)
- Established credentials verifying personal health, character, and professional status.

(5)
- Experienced in public education, private non-profit, and industry child care situations.

- Formal training in a certified public postsecondary institution.

- Proven effectiveness in working with children, parents, educators, and company management — references available. (6)

EXPERIENCE

(7)
1987-Present: Assistant Director of Child Care Program, Amsel Industries, Wilmington, ID

1985-87: Child Care Aide, Main Street Methodist Church, Kinton, ID

1983-85: Teacher's Aide, Johnson Elementary School, Sioux, ID

COMMENTS

(8) Licensed Child Care Worker, Idaho County Board of Commissioners

(9) Health and Personal Background Certified

Member: National Association of Child Care Paraprofessionals
(10)

16. Civil Engineer

WORK HISTORY RESUME

General Strategy

Mr. Choy is an engineer with a substantial list of substantive employment situations that fits the **Work History Resume** format well. With it he is able to convey that he has:

- a broad base of specific civil engineering experiences;

- a long, responsible history of upward movement on a well-defined career ladder;

- the appropriate formal education; and

- an array of career-related short courses that have kept him current.

Specific Points

(1) A **Summary** is appropriate in a long, reasonably detailed work history. It serves to draw out important specifics for preliminary attention.

(2) In a few bulleted statements he sketches the breadth of his experience.

(3) The work history relates an unbroken chain of responsible employment from college through present position.

(4) Quantified technical and supervisory experience lets his importance be adequately appraised.

(5) Mention of successfully dealing with specific environmental problems of his industry marks him as a progressive and sensitive technical manager.

(6) Reporting relationships tend to show relative status and are important in describing your place within an organization.

(7) Being both a competent engineer and a person who can relate to government and community concerns is a plus worth mentioning.

(8) Early experience within a major federal agency vouches for an ability to deal with such institutions successfully.

(9) Verification of holding the basic educational credential of his profession.

(10) Evidence of remaining current in his field by attending specialized training over the course of a long career, offsetting a lack of graduate study.

Winston K. Choy
387 Mililani Street
Honolulu, HI 96813
808-222-9988 (Office)
808-333-9075 (Residence)

① **Summary**

Civil Engineer with extensive infrastructure experience, including:

- Liaison with government and private environmental interests
- 26 years of increasingly responsible field experience
- Federal, state, and private workplace exposure
- Professional continuing education
- Significant design innovations
- Major supervisory roles

②

Experience

<u>June 1985 - Present</u>: **Senior Operating Engineer**, Hawaiian Cane Group, Inc., Honolulu, HI. Ranking civil engineer in charge of field irrigation, infrastructure, and fixtures for the number two sugar cane producer in the Islands. Supervise a staff of 129 professionals, technicians, and workers engaged in the design, installation, and maintenance of systems supporting the planting, growing, and harvesting of the crop on three islands. Directly responsible for conversion from immersion to drip irrigation resulting in savings of 32 million gallons of water per year. Developing mechanically induced, high temperature burn-off techniques to comply with EPA air pollution mandates and residential development complaints. ④

<u>April 1978 - May 1985</u>: **Field Engineer**, Knaurhowser Timber Management Corporation, Pine Coast, NC. Led the engineering team responsible for grading, erosion, and fire control mechanics for a 300,000 acre plot of pulp and timber pines in Coastal North Carolina. Reported to Engineering Group Chief Engineer at Atlanta office. Personally responsible for maintenance and emergency response engineering for the full spectrum of plant maturities. Extensive coordination with local and federal fire resources, EPA regulators, and recreation managers. Successfully settled long standing controversy regarding All Terrain Vehicle (ATV) use on company properties. Supervised engineering and support staff team of 74, approximately two-thirds of them professionals. ⑤

③ <u>January 1969 - March 1978</u>: **Staff Engineer**, California Department of Highways, Palo Alto, CA. One of 47 engineers staffing the expansion of the ⑥ Interstate Highway environmental impact retrofit project. Team effort in developing innovative techniques for correcting undesirable impact of initial engineering on 300 cut and fill sites, 47 bridges, and 3,492 water distribution device faults along the 4,229 coastal highway segments of California Interstate highways. Working level liaison with government and private environmental interests. Led a team of 12 civil engineers and draftsmen. ⑦

<u>June 1967 - December 1968</u>: **Civil Engineer III**, San Mateo County Maintenance Division. Working civil engineer supporting the parks and lands division of the county property maintenance group. Participated in design and approval of contractor implemented projects involving roads and infrastructure serving the county's 398 acre park system and adjoining properties. ⑧

<u>June 1963 - May 1967</u>: **Lieutenant, Army Corps of Engineers**, Fort Belvoir, VA. Junior engineering officer participation on coastal wetlands survey group. Ultimately merged with teams responsible for design and placement of beach erosion devices on the Outer Banks. Supervised a civilian contract construction group.

Education

⑨ Bachelor of Science
Civil Engineering
University of East Texas, 1963

Comments

Participated in a series of applied career related short courses, including:

- 1965 - Army Corps of Engineers Advanced School for Coastal Problem Resolution, Charleston Regional Office, SC.
- 1968 - Environmental Coalition Associations Symposium, Mare Island, CA
- 1970 - Southwestern Highway Engineers Retrofit Annual, Tucson, AZ
- 1973 - Major Contractors' Annual Meeting, San Francisco, CA
- 1974 - The Environment and the Civil Engineer, Lake Louise, AL
- 1978 - Timber Management Engineers Regional Conference, Lumberton, NC
- 1985 - Agricultural Civil Engineering in the 1980s, Great Valley, CA

⑩

17. College Administrator

WORK HISTORY RESUME

General Strategy

Dr. Custer is presenting a detailed and lengthy resume that addresses itself to a specific position. While it is a composite that draws on all three classes, it is predominantly a **Work History Resume.** With it he is able to:

- direct the resume to a specific individual regarding a single position;

- give a great deal of detail about his background in only two pages; and

- separate the resume into components that can be exploited individually without undue effort—detailed **Overview, Experience**, and **Education** sections are supplemented by **Personal** information deemed relevant in this situation (a career crossover from the traditional academic world to a professional recruiting firm).

Specific Points

(1) The resume is personalized to the hiring official and specific position.

(2) The **Overview** evidences comprehensive national experience—plenty of valuable contacts for the professional recruitment firm he aspires to join.

(3) The **Experience** section accounts for all periods of time since college.

(4) Current position emphasizes being in the midst of the professional nerve center for the field in which he will recruit and place people.

(5) Professional award certifies the high regard in which he is held.

(6) Indication of prior private-sector initiatives and experience in his proposed crossover field. Note overlapping dates as this activity was continued privately while holding present position.

(7) More than one position within a single system can be shown this way.

(8) Military career, continued as reserve officer, is another indication of initiative, broader knowledge, and further sources of contacts—networking.

(9) The right collegiate credentials to function at the intended level.

(10) Image appropriate to the position being sought—city and country homes. Acceptable height and weight, stable marriage, etc. might even be added when judged potentially helpful.

Atwell W. Custer

Prepared for the consideration of Michael J. Woodward, President
Academy For the Recruitment of Professionals

Director of Executive Search Position

OVERVIEW

- **Earned doctorate in higher education**

- **19 years of successful experience as an educator**
  - 5 as a national association professional
  - 10 as a college dean
  - 3 as a college counselor
  - 1 as a classroom teacher

- **National college curriculum development and articulation experience**

- **Working knowledge of Washington higher education organizations**

EXPERIENCE

- **January 1983 - Present**: *Associate Director (initially Senior Consulting Specialist), American Association of Public Colleges and Universities (AAPCU), Members Opportunity Colleges (MOC), a joint project with the American Association of Service Colleges (AASC), The Center for Education, Washington, DC.* Work nationally with colleges offering voluntary postsecondary education to the membership community. Act as liaison between the major higher education associations and the community services. Devise degree programs needed by the services and negotiate articulation agreements between the participating colleges. Implement the programs internationally to include training college educators in their use. Extensive consultation with those who direct the colleges, professional associations, and the government agencies involved. Associated budget, management, and data processing responsibilities. Awarded *1984 Outstanding Professional Award* by the AAPCU Board of Directors for efforts in establishing the MOC Associate Degree Program.

- **February 1982 - Present**: *Self-Employed Personnel Consultant.* Established an executive recruiting firm in Charlotte, NC at a time when interest rates and the economic climate made it most unattractive for people to relocate. Faced with the realities of the times and insufficient capital to weather the cycle without supplementary income, I relocated the business to Washington where consulting fees in the higher education and military communities were available while continuing to develop the business by recruiting financial analysts on a part-time basis. With economic recovery the business prospered and continues to provide a substantial share of my income. I was extensively trained by Nelson Executive Search, Inc. as a part of my original franchise operation.

- **July 1968 - February 1982**: *Virginia Community College System, Pine Ridge Community College Campus, Meyers Cave, Virginia*

> *July 1971 - February 1982*: *Dean of Students.* Responsible for counseling, academic advisement, admissions and records, student activities, student rights and responsibilities, faculty liaison, administrative data processing, student financial aid, research and reporting, Equal Opportunity, management information system and CETA program. Extensive involvement in the overall management of the college including the planning and building of Phase III, budgeting, staffing, projecting enrollments, needs assessment, interaction with other agencies, representing the college on numerous VCCS task force projects relating to statewide concerns. Ten years of regional accreditation team participation with SACS at colleges throughout the South.

> *July 1968 - July 1971*: *Counselor.* Responsible for the career and academic advisement of community college students. Selected for full-time doctoral study with pay.

- **September 1967 - June 1968**: *History teacher.* Jaluko School, Hawaii

- **February 1966 - August 1967**: *Full-time graduate study and travel.*

- **June 1962 - Present**: *United States Air Force*

> *June - September 1962*: Officer Training School, Texas; *September 1962 - June 1963*: Photo-Radar Intelligence training, Texas; *July 1963 - January 1966*: Intelligence Officer, Japan & Hawaii; *January 1966 - Present*: Reserve intelligence officer with a variety of assignments throughout the US and the Far East. Currently command a 47 member unit at Langley AFB, VA. Ten years of association with the USAF Academy as a Liaison Officer. Assignments to the Defense Intelligence College including a substantive role in its accreditation by Middle States. Management courses.

EDUCATION

Doctor of Philosophy, 1971, University of Maryland
Student Personnel Administration/Higher Education

Master of Education, 1967, University of Maryland
Counseling and Personnel Services

Bachelor of Science, 1962, Mosshill State College, Maryland
Education/Social and Biological Sciences

PERSONAL

Washington Apartment: 35 New Hampshire Avenue NW #7220
Washington, DC 20036   202-276-9074

Virginia Farm: Route 3, Box 5
Windy Cave, VA 24499   703-224-9861

Office: 800-399-5242/202-299-7071

18. College Professor

FOCUSED RESUME

General Strategy

Ms. Dow is in the process of making the transition to a higher level of functioning in her present specialty—teaching history. The **Focused Resume** gives her the format to present her admirable work history and associated educational credentials, but, importantly, it also lets her focus on her strongest assets outside the context of the setting she wants to move from.

She *focuses* on her:

- objective of moving from the high school to the community college–level institution;

- ability to teach history to anyone, regardless of level or ability; and

- scholarly productivity.

Specific Points

1. An **Objective** statement says in a sentence what she wants to do, at what level, and in what geographic area.

2. Six years of teaching history are documented.

3. Successful part-time experience teaching history at the community college level to which she aspires is demonstrated.

4. Professionalism beyond that expected of a high school history teacher is shown—desirable traits for a college professor and apt to impress those reviewing her resume.

5. Experience recounted in traditional work history fashion.

6. Honors as an outstanding teacher validate her competence.

7. Community outreach project is apt to be a well-regarded initiative at the college level where similar arrangements are valued.

8. Adjunct position shows ability to function on college level with adults.

9. Willingness to teach in a nontraditional setting is potentially important.

10. Being a former community college student looks good for this position.

Cynthia M. Dow

9827 North Millwork Lane
College Park, MD 20740
301-922-9988 (Office)
301-373-9075 (Residence)

 Objective: To obtain a tenure track position teaching U. S. History at the community college level in the Central Atlantic region.

Overview

 • Six years of teaching history at a public high school to a cross-section of different ability level students.

• Three years of teaching history at the community college level on a part-time adjunct faculty basis.

 • Secretary-Treasurer of the Maryland History Teachers Association and active in public outreach historical promotions.

 • Published articles in *Mid-Atlantic History* in 1985 and 1987.

Experience

September 1983 - Present: Teacher of history, Prince George High School, Ableville, MD. Teach U.S. History to top 3 sections of eleventh grade students; World History to 2 mid-level sections of seniors; and 1 section of honors students on Contemporary Policy Issues. Voted teacher of the year twice, first runner-up for Maryland Teacher in 1989. Co-founder of Parents, Students and Business Leaders, a community foundation that raises non-public funds to augment the school budget for special equipment and events.

August 1986 - Present: Concurrent with full-time position noted above, assumed duties as **U.S. History teacher at Johnson County Community College**. Responsible for an evening class of working young adults at the campus and a study-release class of inmates at the college's outreach campus in Stanboard Correctional Institute.

Education

Master of Arts
History
University of Maryland, 1983

Bachelor of Arts
History
Johns Hopkins University, 1982

Associate in Arts
Liberal Arts
Hagerstown Junior College, 1980

19. Computer Operator

FOCUSED RESUME

General Strategy

Ms. Paris has the training and experience to do the job, but she has been out of the workplace for several years. She will use the **Focused Resume** to place the emphasis on specific, enduring skills lifted from the context of her somewhat dated work history.

With this approach she *focuses* on her:

- ability to use either of the two best-known families of computers;
- familiarity with the kinds of software most likely to be encountered in a new position; and
- overall quality of being a good worker in a team setting.

Specific Points

① Since her experience is not current, she begins by documenting her basic formal preparation to do computer work—her education.

② Establishes the fact that the most popular computer systems are familiar.

③ Verifies that she knows the software and can use it in either environment.

④ Traditionally presented work history showing dates of employment.

⑤ Demonstrates that she has continued to be productive using her computer skills even while not employed in a regular position.

⑥ Evidence of being able to coordinate her work with those who generate the input for her computerized efforts.

⑦ Experience with a larger mainframe computer is mentioned to show versatility.

⑧ Ability to work in the absence of immediate on-site supervision.

⑨ Demonstrates ability to do more than just operate equipment.

⑩ Brief explanation of her absence from the workplace.

Elizabeth R. Paris

856 Lincoln Way, Apartment 102
New Orleans, LA 70119
504-363-9075 (Residence)

Education

① Diploma
Data Processing
Dauphine School of Business, 1980

Strengths

②

- Trained in the operation of both IBM and Apple Macintosh families of personal computers and peripherals.

③

- Experienced in word processing, desktop publishing, database management, and spreadsheet software for MS-DOS and Macintosh operating systems.

- Task oriented, independently productive worker with the proven ability to cooperate in team efforts.

Experience

June 1983 - 1985: **Data-entry operator** working from my residence as an independent contractor to major publishers. Enter author prepared text data into book formats using appropriate desktop publishing software on my Macintosh ⑤ computer. Produced 4 books annually for the 3 year period. Excellent evaluations from authors and editors, with whom I coordinated closely. ⑥

④

June 1980 - May 1983: **Computer Operator**, Middlesex County Library, Suffolk, NY. Responsible for the operation of the library's TI-5000 stand alone computer system used in catalog maintenance, ordering, lender record keeping, and ⑦ payroll. Worked under the supervision of the Data Systems Manager who oversaw similar operations in 3 other county ⑧ office complexes. Instrumental in bringing on line the library's first CD units for user research. Assisted in obtaining a Library of Congress grant for that project.

⑨

Comments: I left the workplace in order to be in the home during my child's early years and I now want to return to a traditional career path.

⑩

20. Computer Programmer

WORK HISTORY RESUME

General Strategy

Ms. Leone is an entrepreneurial professional with several years of valuable experience that she wants to present to like-minded people. Since her experience is traditional, in good order, and descriptive of her talents, she appropriately elected to use the **Work History Resume**.

With this presentation she can:

- show what she has to offer and what she aspires to achieve;

- show her detailed work history; and

- comment on her inclination toward participating in a business on a speculative basis.

Specific Points

① Key to her presentation is the fact that she is prepared technically—has the right degree.

② Next she summarizes her dual experience in the manufacturing and user communities.

③ In the **Overview,** she addresses her orientation toward taking a participating position in a high-tech start-up—trading talent for future profits.

④ Documents key systems role with a major applications consumer.

⑤ Describes a large applications project that she oversaw that was commercially successful.

⑥ Uses quantifiable measures of her success in helping the firm make money by using applied computer capabilities.

⑦ Her knowledge made a computer fit the marketplace profitably.

⑧ Experience working in the national systems programming community.

⑨ Bonus as verification of the value of her contributions.

⑩ A brief recap of willingness to take a business risk and what she might contribute to the success of a start-up.

Raye F. Leone

8734 Woodland Avenue
Louisville, KY 40210
502-222-9988 (Office)
502-333-9075 (Residence)

Education

(1)

Bachelor of Science
Information Sciences
Kentucky State College, 1983

Overview

Six years of combined systems and applications programming experience in both the computer manufacturing industry and a major commercial user's organization. *(2)* Degree focus on advanced systems/applications interfaces with summer work-study arrangements at IBX Labs, Palo Alto, CA. Seek stable, entrepreneurial start-up willing to trade ownership participation for exceptional technical contributions. *(3)*

Experience

June 1987 - Present: Director of Computer Applications, Seemans Regional Office Supplies, Louisville, KY. Assumed newly created position with major ($387 million annual sales) regional office supply firm. Tasked with computer order *(5)* *(4)* placement and remote technical support for a field sales force of 143 professionals covering the Southeastern U.S. Successfully acted as systems analyst, applications programmer, and interacted with supplier systems programmers to achieve an industry recognized breakthrough system of laptop/modem support sales. *(6)* Development costs recovered in 16 months. Sales staff turnover reduced 38 percent in last year. Lost sales attributable to support lag reduced to less than 4 percent after 14 months.

June 1983 - May 1987: Systems Programmer, Comtrack Computer Corporation, Waco, TX. Adapted existing personal computer operating systems to fit the unique *(7)* needs of Comtrack's market niche — the traveling technical sales representative. Worked in cooperation with applications programmers in the Seattle and Atlanta *(8)* software markets supporting conversions of popular products to Comtrack operating systems. Successfully programmed a disk conversion system provided with new Comtrack desktops that strengthened advertising and accounted for a substantial share of the firm's $28 million of crossover sales last year. Consistent performance bonuses for outstanding contributions. *(9)*

Comments

Offer a solid base of user and manufacturer experience, excellent technical credentials, and a willingness to take reasoned business risks. *(10)*

21. Computer Sales Representative

FOCUSED RESUME

General Strategy

Mr. Winters is just out of college, has all the right training, and some good part-time experience, but lacks a history of full-time employment. In order to show what his strengths are, he has decided to use a **Focused Resume.**

In this case the *focus* will be on:

- a college education that directly and practically prepared him for technical sales;

- seasonal jobs that have already given him a start in the business; and

- a technical background sufficient to let him sell authoritatively.

Specific Points

1. Specific college training in the technical sales specialty.

2. Identification of the technical sales market segment that he aspires to serve—small-business and personal computers.

3. Demonstrated experience in the business beyond the sales floor.

4. Seasonal sales of relevant software for a nationally franchised outlet.

5. Specific experience dealing with small-computer users as customers.

6. Hands-on technical experience in a laboratory setting—transferable skills include demonstrating computer equipment.

7. Success as a salesperson in the technical market.

8. A practical way to demonstate link between college activities and potential success as a professional in technical sales.

9. Recognition of the career ladder and a motivation to climb it.

10. An understanding of the compensation system and subtle confidence that he will prosper under it.

Roscoe V. Winters
8037 Mahaney Avenue
Norwich, CT 06360
203-345-9075 (Residence)

Education

(1) Associate in Science
Technical Merchandising
Mitchell Community College, 1989

(2) **Objective:** To obtain a technical marketing position with a major retail vendor of personal and small business computers.

Strengths

- Three summers of full-time employment in The Computer Shed, a retail computer outlet of the Systems Computing Corporation of Sunnyvale, CA. Performed backroom assembly, stock maintenance, and *(3)* inventory for their line of desktop and laptop computers.

(4)
- Christmas seasonal employment as a floor sales representative at The Software Place, a nationally franchised purveyor of off-the-shelf applications software to small commercial users and individuals. *(5)*

(6)
- College work-study experience as a computer laboratory assistant to the professor of data processing technology at Mitchell Community College. Spent 15 hours weekly assisting in the set-up and operation of the lab sessions in which students from non-computer disciplines learned the basics of practical computer use.

(7)
- Junior Salesperson of the Year Award 1988, Technical Magazine and *(8)* Book Direct Sales Organization. Award included a $500 tuition grant and was earned by leading the Northeast region in subscription sales on behalf of the Campus Computer Users Club.

Comments

(9) Highly motivated for a career in technical merchandising with aspirations for management after acquiring experience. Planning to pursue continuing education in the related technologies. Receptive to incentive-based compensation. *(10)*

22. Computer Service Technician

WORK HISTORY RESUME

General Strategy

Ms. Nissan has a very strong combination of technical preparation and experience in the workplace. Nothing will do a better job of displaying her desirable qualities than the **Work History Resume.**

With the standard resume, she can show that she:

- seeks a senior position in a specific setting;

- has the technical degree to underwrite her ambitions;

- worked her way up the career ladder to this point; and

- possesses a record of achievement in her specialty.

Specific Points

1. Her **Goal** is one of two job titles whose parameters are known to those who would be examining her resume.

2. She has a particular set of geographic limitations and says so.

3. The degree she has is well matched to her field and is highlighted.

4. **Overview** sketches length and type of experience plus it verifies that she has continued her education in the most desirable of ways for this field.

5. **Experience** gives the chronology of a well-executed march up the career ladder in the computer service field.

6. Position quantitatively bracketed to describe magnitude of responsibilities.

7. Success demonstrated by commendations and tangible proof of expanded contract base attributable to her performance.

8. Effectively sketches the reporting relationship, size, and nature of the work situation.

9. Specific, measurable results are given when verifiable by references.

10. Hands-on entry-level experience resulted in success that is decribed here both technically and in terms of customer satisfaction—a plus in any service business.

Lynn T. Nissan

692 Alpine Avenue
Denver, CO 80203
303-222-9988 (Office)
303-333-9075 (Residence)

Goal: Service Manager or Senior Customer Engineer for a contract maintenance firm serving the business computer market of the Denver/Boulder/Colorado Springs corridor.

Education

 Associate in Science
Electronics Technology
Denver County Junior College, 1981

Overview: Six years of progressively more responsible service positions with manufacturers, service contractors, and major computer users in the Mountain Region. Extensive specialized training at manufacturers' schools.

Experience

<u>October 1987 - Present</u>: <u>Customer Engineer</u>, Wilmac Computer Services Corporation, Cherry Creek, CO. Technical service representative for Wilmac (13th largest contractor of its kind in the U.S.) providing liaison between manufacturers and users on the warranty service backing installations of $500,000 and more in aggregate value. Responsible for the installation, maintenance, troubleshooting, and fulfillment aspects of operating equipment in 4 western states. Consistently received manufacturers' commendations for excellence of support and efficient problem resolution. Increased contract volume by 27 percent in region during the period.

 <u>March 1983 - September 1987</u>: <u>Computer Service Coordinator</u>, Rocky Mountain National Bank, Denver, CO. Reported directly to the Director of Computer Services for the 23 office system of financial services computers including ATM, EFT, and overall accounting/audit program support. Responsible for the installation and maintenance of computer supported equipment. Supervised a crew of 6 technicians performing maintenance and repairs under my direction with the assistance of manufacturers' service reps when appropriate. Reduced downtime by 35 percent during my first 10 months on the job. Extended replacement intervals on key equipment components by 77 percent over my tenure.

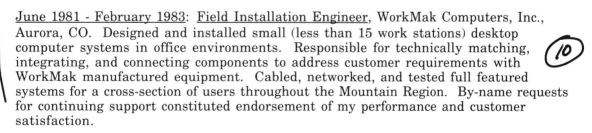 <u>June 1981 - February 1983</u>: <u>Field Installation Engineer</u>, WorkMak Computers, Inc., Aurora, CO. Designed and installed small (less than 15 work stations) desktop computer systems in office environments. Responsible for technically matching, integrating, and connecting components to address customer requirements with WorkMak manufactured equipment. Cabled, networked, and tested full featured systems for a cross-section of users throughout the Mountain Region. By-name requests for continuing support constituted endorsement of my performance and customer satisfaction.

23. Computer Systems Analyst

FOCUSED RESUME

General Strategy

Ms. Alamitos has a lot of strengths and she can demonstrate achievement, but it comes across more boldly if extracted from the four relatively brief periods of employment that constitute her work history. Her best bet is to use the **Focused Resume** in order to concentrate the reviewers' attention on her strong points and not make them dig it out of the several places where she acquired it.

Her correct choice of resume will present her as someone with:

- a strong educational background for being an analyst;
- experience that spans several important user-group industries;
- valuable familiarity with systems of great commercial potential; and
- a set of significant achievements as a systems analyst.

Specific Points

① Her combination of degrees is particularly strong and worth highlighting.

② **Overview** emphasizes that ideal preparation and adds her broad, if brief, experience in large-market industries—also names the position she wants in terms readily understood in her specialty.

③ Specific industry groups and perspectives detailed.

④ A popular systems specialty is mentioned as an attractive strength.

⑤ Gives practical application to her dual-track education.

⑥ Award indicates success and offsets short tenure in the position.

⑦ A specific project with tangible results achieved.

⑧ A systems analysis case history in capsule form.

⑨ Employment gives a chronology of significant positions.

⑩ Summary format provides dates, but after strengths and achievements have already been made clear—instead of along with them as would have been the case in a work history resume, for example.

Louise S. Alamitos

8231 Fairway Drive
Costa Mesa, CA 92627
714-222-9988 (Office)
714-333-9075 (Residence)

Education

Associate in Science
Computer Sciences
Palomar Junior College, 1980

Bachelor of Science
Business Administration
California State University, 1982

 Overview: Rigorous business training backed by legitimate technical credentials in computer sciences. Experienced in major industry segments of business systems analysis including banking, government, and manufacturing. Seek Lead Analyst position with services company catering to a cross-section of such clients.

Strengths

 • Broad systems experience across the government, defense contractor, commercial and consumer banking industries.

• Perspectives of government contract review authorities, major industry bidders, and funding sources.

 • Expert system forecasting models developed in environments targeting companies, agencies, and individual consumers.

• Outstanding ability to extract and relate requirements to non-systems managers and decision makers.

 • Knowledge of computer and business fields enhances ability to convey business system requirements to computer programmers.

Achievements

 • Commerce Department Junior Analyst of the Year Award, 1983, for contributions to advanced industry sampling model.

 • RWC bonus system restructured on the basis of cost-benefit analysis conducted by my project group resulting in reallocation of 73 percent of middle-management bonus dollars.

• Billing errors reduced by 39 percent and customer complaints reduced 78 percent at SuperCard after sampling-based analysis of historical problems data revealed correctable procedural errors.

Employment

Senior Analyst, Card Services Division, SuperCard, Inc., San Francisco, CA, December 1987 - Present.

Systems Analyst, Bank of the West, San Diego, CA, June 1985 - November 1987.

Specifications Analyst, Rocket Weapons Corporation, Reston, VA, July 1984 - May 1985.

Junior Systems Analyst, U.S. Department of Commerce, Washington, DC, June 1982 - June 1984.

24. Corrections Officer

WORK HISTORY RESUME

General Strategy

Mr. Gregg has a logical progression of jobs in the law enforcement and security areas that are easily described in the traditional **Work History Resume** format. What he has done relates directly to the job on which it was done and this approach to describing his abilities will:

- show that he is trained for security work;

- verify in specific settings that he has gained valuable experience that relates directly to his occupational objective; and

- convey the unique nature of his circumstances and just what he is trying to achieve.

Specific Points

1. He has formal postsecondary training at the college level in the corrections field that matches his goal directly—a strong point worthy of prominence.

2. Since he is seeking another federal job, it is relevant to establish that he is already on the register—a part of the federal employment system.

3. His experience as a security officer—shift supervision in a secure environment—is compatible with the corrections job he seeks.

4. A responsible position, related to his field and indicative of good character.

5. Jail house supervision is relevant and worth mentioning.

6. Experience in prison disturbance control is also a strength to note.

7. Honorable military service is a plus in his line of work.

8. Guard duty, even in a diplomatic setting, has relevance for the job sought.

9. **Comments** is a good place to explain his situation briefly—in case the cover letter gets separated from the resume.

10. No concern about privacy since a change is mandated, so he correctly asks that his resume be passed along to anyone who might be able to help him.

Thomas G. Gregg
8309 Agassette Circle
Dobbs Ferry, NY 10522
914-222-9988 (Office)
914-333-9075 (Residence)

Education

① Associate in Science
Corrections
Myrth Valley Community College, 1979

Employment

③ <u>June 1987 - Present</u>: Security Officer, Meredith Air Force Base, NY. GS-9 position as an Air Force civilian law enforcement officer charged with maintaining gate security. Supervise a shift consisting of 6 USAF enlisted security police and 2 civilians.

④ <u>June 1983 - May 1987</u>: Deputy Sheriff, Grapevine County Sheriffs Department, NY. Performed general duties in a mid-sized, rural law enforcement organization. Obligations included serving court papers, crowd and traffic control, and supervision of the county jail, as one of ⑤ three officers on rotation. Augmented prison authorities in controlling major disturbance at Northern State Prison in 1985. ⑥

⑦ <u>July 1979 - May 1983</u>: United States Marine Corps, Quantico, VA. Served as an enlisted combat Marine. Left active-duty as a Corporal selected for Sergeant, a rank assumed in the Reserve.   Experience included two years as an embassy security guard in Europe. ⑧

⑨ **Comments:** Due to the general reduction of forces occurring internationally, Meredith AFB is scheduled for deactivation in the spring. I am in interested in transitioning to a law enforcement position within a federal corrections institution. A completed Form 171 and references are available upon request. Please feel free to share this resume with other agencies. ⑩

25. Credit Manager

WORK HISTORY RESUME

General Strategy

Mr. Masden has an array of work experiences that serve to verify his preparation for the next step on his career ladder. The **Work History Resume** is ideal for showcasing his steady rise in this conservative line of employment.

His resume will show that he:

- has made the necessary career steps to assume a more responsible position in the same line of work.

- has a college degree and has compensated for its nonbusiness nature by taking a number of specialized courses in his occupational field.

Specific Points

1. A terse **Summary** is all that is needed to set the stage for his presentation, which simply says: "I'm ready for the next step."

2. The stature of his current employer is established in order to convey his own responsibilities impressively.

3. It is important to indicate the kinds of client companies that he has experience analyzing.

4. Implementing systematic procedures was a specific and successful practice that he was responsible for and it is properly mentioned—with results.

5. Even more dramatic bottom-line savings are shown by this example of his work.

6. A brief but understandable picture of his credit analysis experience at the bank.

7. Knowledge gained in this position has obvious value in future credit analysis roles, so that is implied in this entry.

8. A responsible entry-level position in credit analysis.

9. A less-than-ideal college degree is noted, but not emphasized.

10. His strong suit is specialized training courses within the credit industry.

Edmund S. Masden

784 East Main Street
Cheyenne, WY 82009
307-222-9988 (Office)
307-333-9075 (Residence)

 Summary: Experienced credit manager seeking growth opportunity.

Experience

June 1987 - Present: Credit Manager, Watkins Wholesale Restaurant Supply, Greensboro, WY.   Responsible for data collection, interviews, analysis, and credit approval recommendations for a $4.5 million annual sales wholesaler. Clients include national franchise, small start-up, and established traditional restaurants and institutions.   Default rate reduced 39 percent during the second year of implementing National Credit Rating Standards procedures under my direction. Implemented Quick-Screen, a procedure for preempting poor risks without the inefficiency of extensive application and credit analysis — resulting in savings averaging $14,000 per quarter for the past 18 months.

June 1983 - May 1987: Credit Analyst, Bank of Northwest Wyoming, Suffolk, WY. Worked as the main officer analyst of small business and consumer credit applications. Maintained a case load of 45 active files per week, resolving 80 percent within that time frame. Knowledge of credit network protocols and ability to digest elaborate business plans quickly.   Supported the lending efforts of 6 commercial and 9 consumer lenders.

July 1979 - May 1983: Credit Clerk, Wilcoxson Consumer Finance, North Woods, WY. Assisted the local office manager and secretary in the operation of a store-front consumer lending business. Took credit applications from walk-in clients and conducted rapid credit checks to approve high-risk/low-amount unsecured consumer loans.

Formal Education

BA, Art History
Smith University, 1983

Specialized Credit Training

- 1983 — Two week training session at the American Consumer Training Academy, Washington, DC, in basic credit analysis.
- 1984-85— Completed the correspondence version of the National Credit Association's Basic and Intermediate Credit Management Courses and earned their Certified Credit Manager (CCM) designation.
- 1987 — Advanced Credit Analysis and Management Course, Wholesale Merchants of America, 2 weeks of resident and 6 months of correspondence learning, Chicago, IL.

26. Customer-Service Representative

FOCUSED RESUME

General Strategy

Ms. Falls has been out of the regular workplace for many years and wants to present her assets outside the context of chronologically listed jobs. The best format for her situation is the **Focused Resume** because it will allow her to:

- make a pointed case for an accumulation of valuable experiences gained outside the traditional workplace;

- show that she can demonstrate achievements there that are relevant to potential success in the full-time job she now seeks; and

- present herself as a worthwhile applicant with the motivation, training, and ability to succeed in a regular position after a long absence.

Specific Points

① A strong **Summary** says it all briefly, but convincingly enough to get the reviewer to read on to the specifics of what she has to offer.

② Her planned transition is designed to take full advantage of current skills in telephone-based sales and services.

③ A core of retail merchandising experience is timeless and a valuable base.

④ Volunteer work on a local telephone hotline is relevant experience.

⑤ More valuable is her home-based telemarketing of commercial services.

⑥ Productivity vouched for by incentive awards.

⑦ Further evidence of initiative and effectiveness as a persuasive telephone personality.

⑧ Weak employment history seems less important after the relevant strengths have already been extracted and sold in the preceding parts of the resume.

⑨ Initiative to get a current education in merchandising is a good endorsement of attitude and potential, plus assurance that she knows the latest trends and terms.

⑩ A closing word of explanation that clarifies situation and goal.

Kathleen T. Falls
3179 MacCline Street
Milwaukee, WI 53203
414-333-9075 (Residence)

Summary

 Woman with formal training in merchandising returning to workplace after 18 years as full-time housewife. Seeking a telephone customer service/sales representative position with a national retailer to build on base of successful, current, part-time telemarketing experience.

Relevant Experience

 • Five years as a retail clerk and department head for F. A. Olson Department Stores, Milwaukee, WI.

• Suicide Hotline of Montgomery County telephone volunteer for 6 years.

 • Home-based telephone marketing person for *SignCard* of Wisconsin for 34 months selling credit card registry, buyers club, and private club privileges to gold card holders.

Accomplishments

 • Won three incentive trips during as many years in peripheral bank card services telemarketing.

 • Voted Volunteer of the Quarter for the community hotline dealing with teen suicide potentials.

Work History

1986 - Present: Part-time telemarketing person with *SignCard* of Wisconsin, Wisconsin State Bank, Milwaukee, WI.

1971 - 1989: Full-time housewife and mother with heavy involvement in community affairs.

1966 - 1971: Retail sales and department manager, F. A. Olson Department Stores, Milwaukee, WI.

Education

Certificate
Merchandising
Milwaukee Community College, 1989

Comments: Never far removed from the mainstream of commercial and community activity during the raising of my family, I returned to college during the past year to ensure currency in my skills. Highly motivated to build a successful full-time telemerchandising career now that time is available.

27. Dental Assistant and Hygienist

WORK HISTORY RESUME

General Strategy

Ms. Wilkinson is applying for a paraprofessional position within a narrow, well-defined specialty. Her training and experience are nicely conveyed in the traditional **Work History Resume** even though her employment record is relatively brief.

Her resume will be used to:

- highlight the special educational preparation;

- note her professional certification; and

- show a record of successfully applying her talents and defining a specialty.

Specific Points

1. **Seeking** quickly frames the limits of what she wants to do and where.

2. The applied degree in dental assisting from an accredited program is a strong asset worth placing at the top of her list of qualifications.

3. Professional certification is almost more valuable than a degree in many specialties—it constitutes approval to practice and a valued measure of job competency.

4. Experience is very specific in this case and lends itself to point-by-point statements.

5. Portrayal of the size and specialized nature of the practice she supports.

6. Statement of the kinds of procedures performed is especially necessary, considering her goal.

7. Describes how she has prepared for the specialty—vendor schools valued.

8. The extent of her interest in advanced technology use is conveyed by mentioning the latest computer simulation and design procedures.

9. Specific professional references are essential here and they are listed.

10. A brief, easily understood reason for leaving is given in closing.

Cher W. Wilkinson

1123 Marshall Avenue
Shepherdstown, WV 25443
304-222-9988 (Office)
304-333-9075 (Residence)

 Seeking: Full-time position with an institutional dental plan or health management organization in the greater Washington area having an advanced cosmetic dentistry practice.

Education

Associate in Applied Science
 Dental Technology
Huntington Junior College, 1983

ADA Board Certified
Cosmetic Dental Assistant (CDA)
1987

Experience

April 1985 - Present:

- Dental Assistant in a one doctor family practice.
- In the past 18 months it grew from 10 percent to 68 percent cosmetic dentistry clients.
- Primarily bleach and bonding, with increasing attention to porcelain caps and reconstructive alterations.
- Extensive reading and attendance at vendor-sponsored workshops on the lastest cosmetic dentistry assisting techniques.
- Routinely assist in acid-prep cleaning and heat finishing of final applications.
- Trained and experienced in aesthetic approximations technology and related computer modeling where CAD/CAM applications are being used in the preparation of dental prostheses.

Reference: Ruth A. Flausmun, D.D.S., College Park Professional Center, Suite 305, Sheppardstown, WV 25442, 304-222-9988.

June 1983 - March 1985:

- Traditional dental assisting position in a two doctor practice.
- Prepare materials for various treatments.
- Take and develop X-rays.
- Chair-side assistance in standard practices.
- Cleaning and scaling.

Reference: William J. Schwartz, D.D.S., Johnson & Schwartz, P.C., 309 Middletown Pike, Hagerstown, MD 22501, 301-743-9099.

Comments: Present employer relocating her practice to California.

28. Editor

WORK HISTORY RESUME

General Strategy

Ms. Jason has a solid record of traditional workplace experience in her profession and it can be well presented in the **Work History Resume.**

She uses the resume to accomplish:

- an effective **Overview** of her experience;

- a detailed enumeration of duties in various positions;

- a suitable college degree; and

- **comments** that relate her special orientation and goal.

Specific Points

1. The New York address has significance in certain fields—publishing is one.

2. Her work is described sufficiently in the **Overview** to allow efficient screening by other professionals in her business.

3. **Experience** in her case is an objective detailing of times, tasks, and firms.

4. Quantification is important even in the arts—it defines level of responsibility and places achievements in a meaningful context.

5. A signal accomplishment is a strong way to end a particular job description.

6. Similarly quantified achievement portrays work in another setting.

7. Showing specific instances of measurable success strengthens credibility.

8. Verification that she performed well at the working level before entering the higher echelons of editorial work.

9. A worthy college background for an editorial career.

10. **Comments** frame her real objective and distinguish her for those entrepreneurial publishers she has decided to target with her resume.

Christine A. Jason

873 West 49th Street
New York, NY 10019
212-222-9988 (Office)
212-333-9075 (Residence)

①

Overview

② More than a decade of successful editorial experience in trade book divisions of national and regional presses. Outstanding record of productivity in acquisitions, development, and market penetration.

③ Experience

June 1987 - Present: *Executive Editor, Business Books Division, Delconte & Sons, Inc., New York, NY.* Supervise 12 acquisitions and developmental editors and a supporting staff of 18 individuals, 9 professional and 9 clerical. Responsible for bringing Delconte ④ into the modern era of published how-to-do-it books for the small business market. Increased market share by 47 percent in last 14 months. Products of this division opened airport and mass discount retailers to Delconte books where sales now account ⑤ for 15 percent of the firm's gross sales.

June 1983 - May 1987: *Senior Editor, Bicycle Books, Inc., Irvine, CA.* Managed the ⑥ acquisitions editing division of this New Age regional press generating an average of 23 new trade titles annually in the career choice and health foods niches that constitute its areas of specialization. Highly successful in efforts to identify fresh ideas among first- time authors and generate successful books using developmental editing ⑦ techniques. Ratio of break-even titles increased from 2-in-3 to 7-in-8 during my tenure.

July 1979 - May 1983: *Project Managing Editor, Multi-Title Press, Inc., New York, NY.* Worked as a developmental editor in the new author acquisitions department of the ⑧ paperback trade division of the number 3 seller of such books nationally. Participated in the successful development of such solid national sellers as J. K. Wilson and Carol Minor Jones.

June 1978 - June 1979: World travel following college graduation.

⑨ Education

Bachelor of Arts
Liberal Arts
Metropolitan University, NY 1978

Comments: Primarily interested in acquiring participating status in a contemporary trade start-up or small house with potential for specialized growth in association with aggressive national distributor. Entrepreneurial orientation and financially positioned to consider delayed compensation for the right opportunity.

⑩

29. Electronic Engineer

COMPETENCY CLUSTER RESUME

General Strategy

Mr. VanGogh has a powerful combination of operational and research-and-development experiences that are best presented in a **Competency Cluster Resume.** His particular goal is to make the transition from the military to the civil aviation side of the industry and his most convincing case is made by addressing aggregates of talent valued in both sectors.

His resume is structured to show:

- solid college credentials in his specialized technical field;

- specific, successful experience in three major competency areas;

- achievements that would be meaningful anywhere in the industry;

- a record of continuous employment in the field; and

- a brief statement reaffirming his objective and why it makes sense.

Specific Points

(1) Address has relevance in this case since the civil aviation industry is largely found in the Seattle area—he is available without relocation expenses.

(2) College degrees clearly relate to the professional goal and establish him as a qualified applicant.

(3) Tells how he has implemented successful applications.

(4) Credible as a manager with quantified measures of his experience.

(5) Implications of familiarity with federal regulators and space technology.

(6) Important operational experience adds to technical preparation.

(7) An example of applying military knowledge to a civil aviation application.

(8) Tangible evidence of excellence in his work.

(9) A respectable work history that accounts for all time periods since college.

(10) **Comments** concludes his personal presentation with the goal statement.

Robert P. VanGogh
284 Chanute Lake Drive
Bellevue, WA 98009

206-222-9988 (Office)
206-333-9075 (Residence)

Education

Bachelor of Science
Electrical Engineering
University of Seattle, 1980

Master of Science
Electronic Systems Engineering
University of Seattle, 1986

Applications Experience

- Used night flying and terrain avoidance radar systems as an operational crew member flying F-4s in all weather simulated combat environments.
- Revised Huguenot calibration procedures for standardization of LanSat-based night navigation equipment on transport aircraft.
- Implemented total auto-pilot integration sub-sets for all J-79 systems in use, military and civilian, during the mid-1980s.

Managerial Experience

- Led a team of 4 engineers and 5 technicians supervising the installation of retrofit SatSys decoders on the commercial passenger fleet of Divided Airlines, Inc. over a period of 17 months.
- Quality assurance engineer in charge of 35 technical inspectors in the Final Phase Division of Wilson & Bell Avionics responsible for satisfying FAA mandates on all KeyStat installations.

Research and Development Experience

- Flew debugging missions as an EWO in F-4 aircraft for the operational testing and calibration of BV-3 Birdseye radar systems during their first all weather night tests.
- Master's thesis focus was an unclassified cross-talk translation of military to civilian night wind shear avoidance systems.
- Developed first solid state blind-flight ergometer with sufficient deviation tolerance to satisfy FAA and military STANBOARDS.

Achievements

- Twice received the USAF Commendation medal for contributions to night flying safety, first as an active-duty aviator, then as a contract engineer.
- Reduced material costs 86 percent on EWSD's crossover shear detection night goggles by implementing first industry use of SeepTAC-4 in such applications.
- Secured 14 contracts with a total value of $83 million during 6 years as a contractor's engineer.

Employment

November 1988 - Present: Senior Engineer, Wilson & Bell Avionics Corporation, Bellevue, WA.

June 1986 - October 1988: Project Engineer, Electronic Warfare Systems Division, Elliot Systems, Inc., Los Angeles, CA.

September 1985 - May 1986: Full-time graduate study.

June 1980 - August 1985: Lieutenant, United States Air Force. Electronics Warfare Officer, F-4 Phantom, Tactical Air Command.

Comments: Objective is to make the transition from aerial weapons systems applications to civil aviation. Experience and training in non-visual systems is universal to both sectors.

30. Emergency Medical Technician

Work History Resume

General Strategy

Ms. Ward is creating her resume to obtain a teaching job in the field in which she is now a practitioner. Since her employment has been in a logical career pattern and it describes her strengths well within the context of the jobs held, she is advised to use the **Work History Resume** format.

Her resume will feature her:

- education and certification for a specialized service;

- six years of experience actually practicing her paramedical skills; and

- efforts to make the crossover to teaching.

Specific Points

(1) The EMT associate degree is the key to her training and is featured prominently.

(2) **Overview** is used for the dual purpose of noting professional certification and previewing her work history.

(3) **Experience** accounts for all periods of time and distinguishes full and part-time positions clearly for the reviewer.

(4) Position and job title describe her duties fully to those who know the field.

(5) Level of responsibilities within that position need further amplification that is given by noting team rank and describing duties beyond the expected.

(6) Position is self-descriptive to those familiar with the region's services.

(7) Amplification includes team size and precise mission, including breaking down categories of response.

(8) Part-time experience especially relevant since it represents the desired crossover.

(9) The award for valor adds stature in this business.

(10) Goal clarification and statement of moral commitment to the helping profession.

Dorothy L. Ward

783 Shoreline Drive
Newport News, VA 23606
804-222-9988 (Office)
804-333-9075 (Residence)

Education

① Associate in Applied Science
Emergency Medical Technology
Hampton Area Community College, 1983

② Overview

Board certified Emergency Medical Technician with 6 years
of urban mobile trauma unit response experience.

Experience

<u>Full-time</u>:

④ June 1987 - Present: *Emergency Medical Technician, Eastern
Beach Community Rescue Team*, Eastern Beach, VA. Response ⑤
vehicle team captain assigned to street duties similar to
those described below, but with approximately one-third of
time devoted to dispatcher training and assistance in
telephone administered trauma management.

⑥ June 1983 - May 1987: *Emergency Medical Technician, Woodside
Fire and Rescue Service*, Tidewater, VA. Member of a two- ⑦
③ person response team answering calls in a 300 square block
segment of Southeast Tidewater. Emergencies attended
included 34 percent vehicle accidents, 48 percent violent
crime, 9 percent drug overdoses, and 9 percent routine
medical emergencies such as heart attacks and illnesses.

<u>Part-time</u>:

⑧ October 1985 - Present: *Instructor* of American Red Cross
advanced First Aid, Cardio-Pulmonary Resuscitation (CPR), and
EMT certification training at Bayside Community College
during the fall and spring terms.

Comments

⑨ Recipient of the Governor's Award for Lifesaving as a result
of 1984 recovery and resuscitation of automobile accident
drowning victim.

Reason for Leaving

Seeking a full-time teaching position where my skills
and experience can be conveyed to others.

⑩

31. Employment Counselor

COMPETENCY CLUSTER RESUME

General Strategy

Mr. Richards has mixed two types of employment—business and public. He is crafting a resume that will help him take the best of both and gain a position in the private sector that will satisfy both his love of counseling and desire to profit. In his situation, the **Competency Cluster Resume** will make the strongest case by presenting his most attractive attributes apart from their somewhat restrictive settings.

His resume will describe:

- his education;

- the clusters of business and counseling skills he has acquired; and

- how he now wants to pull them together as an executive recruiter.

Specific Points

1. The degrees show the counselor side of his assets.

2. **Objective** says he is more complex than his education indicates—he has both business and counseling interests and sees how to combine them profitably.

3. The first competency cluster to establish is business and sales—this will balance any skepticism about him being an academic not hardened to the business world.

4. Counseling experience is put in the context of the employment marketplace.

5. Again, a link is established between counseling and job seekers.

6. Implication that he can bring desirable professionalism to recruiting.

7. State licensure verified.

8. Specialized licensure relevant to recruiting is noted.

9. Both counseling and business experience are established by employment record.

10. Goal expresses motivation for the change.

Perry L. Richards
891 Triad Square
Montpelier, VA 23192
804-222-9988 (Office)
804-333-9075 (Residence)

Education

Bachelor of Arts
Psychology
Southern University, 1983

Master of Education
Counseling
Maryland University, 1987

Objective

To apply professional training, licensure, and combined counseling/business experience
to a fee-based position in a professional executive recruitment organization.

• **Business Experience**

Four years as a professional marketing representative for a major pharmaceutical firm. Interacted heavily with professional clients and business associates.

• **Counseling Experience**

Two years as a full-time counselor with the Virginia Employment Service. Counseled adults on job opportunities and assisted arranging training, interviews, the preparation of resumes, and good work practices. One of 9 counselors in a rapidly expanding urban job market. Most clients were high school graduates with little technical or business training or experience.

• **Training**

Psychology degree augmented by a master's degree in educational counseling with a concentration on employment counseling.

• **Supervision**

Practicum experience in master's program consisted of 600 hours of supervision by fully certified professional counselor in an Employment Service Office. Administered in accordance with the requirements for Virginia licensure.

• **Licensure**

Licensed Professional Counselor, Virginia Board of Professional Counselors, General certification with specialization in Employment Counseling. Initially licensed in May 1988.

Certified Personnel Counselor (CPC), National Association of Personnel Consultants, Alexandria, VA.

Employment

<u>June 1987 - Present</u>:   Employment Counselor, Virginia Employment Commission, Mount Scenario, VA.

<u>June 1983 - May 1987</u>:   Medical Sales Representative, Lampton & Boxworth Pharmaceuticals, Inc., Baltimore, MD.

<u>June 1983 - May 1987</u>:   Full-time graduate study.

Comments: Entrepreneurial inclination and strong interest in the private sector motivate me to adapt my counseling and occupational choice training to a career in executive recruitment. Seek commission-based incentive pay not available in institutional counseling settings.

32. Environmental Technician

WORK HISTORY RESUME

General Strategy

Mr. Lee has a set of experiences that conform to the positions and time periods in which they were acquired. In the absence of strong assets that would stand out as aggregate qualities, he is advised to present himself in the context of the standard **Work History Resume.**

His employment history will reveal:

- a candidate looking for an environmental position in the private sector;

- a work history that stems from a logical beginning and progresses through contemporary environmental issues; and

- the basic technical education to support his professional efforts.

Specific Points

① **Introduction** serves as a headline stating who he is and what he wants.

② Experience relates an unbroken chain of employment dating from college graduation.

③ Current position is public, but presented in such a manner as to appeal to developers—his target job market.

④ Specific reference is made to future residential development projects.

⑤ More evidence of competency in the region's environmental concerns.

⑥ Notes that his efforts have produced profit centers for his employers in the past—the test he developed continues to earn money for the consulting firm.

⑦ Shows that he can think like a regulator—he has been one.

⑧ Chemistry teaching is a logical springboard for environmental employment.

⑨ The right degree is presented—no elaboration needed.

⑩ A career value judgment is communicated in his reason-for-leaving statement—he is more comfortable in the private sector and wants to establish himself there.

Winston K. Lee

45 Harriston Boulevard
Ogden, UT 84404
801-222-9988 (Office)
801-333-9075 (Residence)

 Introduction

Experienced environmental scientist seeking private sector position.

Experience

1987 - Present  Environmentalist III, U. S. Environmental Protection Agency, Ogden Field Office, Ogden, UT. GS-13 scientist participating in an industry/river management project in North Snake Development Region. Major project management responsibilities. Benchmarks being established for luxury recreational development communities. Template analysis initiated at outset under my direction.

1983 - 1987   Environmental Consultant, Eco-Systems Consulting Corporation, Denver, CO. Consulting chemist working in conjunction with engineers on the correction of mining-related pollution problems in southern Colorado. Devised tests and neutralization procedures that are now proprietary and constitute standards in the industry.

1980 - 1983   Staff Environmentalist, Oregon Department of Fish and Wildlife, Portland, OR. One of three scientists monitoring industries for compliance with state regulations regarding the discharge of materials potentially harmful to wildlife. Visual inspection and chemical testing of suspicious effluents.

1976 - 1980   Chemistry Teacher, Portland High School, Portland, OR. Instructor of general chemistry.

Education

Bachelor of Science
Chemistry
Utah State University, 1976

Reason for Leaving: Desire to return to private sector employment either in a consulting capacity or as an employee of an environmentally sensitive real estate development firm.

33. Financial Analyst

WORK HISTORY RESUME

General Strategy

Ms. Robinette has selected the **Work History Resume** to present her string of responsible positions in the investment management profession. With it she will attempt to convey that she:

- has the right degrees and professional certification;

- currently holds one of a series of impressive positions in her field; and

- knows when it is time to move on.

Specific Points

① College majors are relevant in a specialized field such as finance.

② Professional certification is a benchmark in institutional investment firms.

③ **Experience** is presented straightforwardly with connecting dates and a full description of duties related to each position.

④ Since her job market is national, she describes the dollar size of her present department so those unfamiliar can better judge her status.

⑤ Details can be tersely presented and still say a lot within an industry group —types of clients, investment orientation, etc. quickly categorize a financial analyst.

⑥ Most organizations value business development (selling) skills, so mention them.

⑦ Computer literacy is essential and it is wise to verify it.

⑧ Short tenure in this position is explained—references would verify.

⑨ Other rather standard duties duly noted on her way up the career ladder.

⑩ Comments used to communicate two important points: (1) She is realistic about heading for a more favorable economic climate, and (2) her performance as a money manager will be of interest so it is volunteered.

Darlene W. Robinette

96 Galveston Lane
Houston, TX 77071
713-222-9988 (Office)
713-333-9075 (Residence)

Education

Bachelor of Science
Business Administration
Smith University, 1965

Master of Business Administration
Finance
University of Texas, 1976

Chartered Financial Analyst (CFA)
1981

Experience

<u>April 1983 - Present</u>: **Vice President & Trust Investment Officer, National Bank & Trust of Eastern Texas, Houston, TX ($1.5 billion trust department)**. Senior portfolio manager in a group of 6; managing both fixed and equity in collective and other funds (personal, pension, and endowment). Responsible for all fixed income funds (aprx $300 million personal/$100 million employee benefits); responsible for most equity funds (aprx $400 million personal/$20 million employee benefits); foundations and charities account for an additional $75 million. Involved in business development activities, including presentations to support new business and existing accounts — also cooperative development projects with other elements of the trust department. Handled installation of IBM-AT dedicated to investment function; computer literate and proficient with DOS, LOTUS, asset allocation programs, Microscan, LOTUS Financial, Norton Utilities, communications, and disk maintenance.

<u>June 1982 - March 1983</u>: **Vice President & Trust Investment Officer, United Bankshares Trust, Fort Worth, TX ($580 million trust department)**. Chaired the investment committee. Lowered transaction costs 32 percent. Implemented standard investment procedures. Established a research capability and client newsletter. Brief tenure accrues to inability to adapt to the culture and lifestyle of the area.

<u>July 1979 - May 1982</u>: **Assistant Vice President and Trust Investment Officer, Chicago Retail Trust Bank, Chicago, IL ($250 million trust department)**. Senior investment officer responsible for setting overall investment posture; conceived and implemented a new common trust fund, revised others. Organized and conducted investment conference for 200 members of the local professional community. Implemented formal procedures to control commission use and allocation. Established investment management goals, including performance measurement techniques. Wrote monthly economic/investment commentary for distribution to 300 regional bankers, government officials, corporate officers and selected clients.

<u>Eight previous years</u>: **Retail stockbroker**, Scott & Delmonico, Inc., Milwuakee, WI.

Comments: <u>Reason for leaving</u> relates to the declining economy of the region where oil, gas, and space programs show little promise in the near future. <u>Investment performance</u> for the past five years: 14th percentile equities; 23rd percentile fixed income; 19th percentile combined.

34. Food Technologist

FOCUSED RESUME

General Strategy

Mr. Boyd has held a series of positions in the food processing industry, but wants to stress his particular strengths rather than just describe each job. The recommended format for this is the **Focused Resume.**

Using this resume vehicle he will be able to *focus* on:

- special capabilities that he has developed that would be of value across the industry;

- several substantial achievements; and

- an overall work history into which these highlights logically fit.

Specific Points

① The ideal degree for his specialty is noted.

② Professional certification is valuable—often can offset graduate study.

③ **Overview** states what he has to offer—stresses production *and* R & D.

④ **Capabilities** are the statement of aggregate skills that might get lost when spread across the several jobs in which they were acquired.

⑤ Familiarity and success in dealing with government in this regulated industry.

⑥ Language capability important in this business.

⑦ Sensitivity to marketing concerns is an asset as he aspires to higher, more general management positions.

⑧ Specific evidence of excellence and quantified, verifiable savings are strong points.

⑨ Had a team-member role in establishing an industry standard—mention it.

⑩ The work history stands alone, now that the strengths have been extracted and presented with emphasis in their own right.

Donald C. Boyd

78 Overton Way
Memphis, TN 38112
901-222-9988 (Office)
901-333-9075 (Residence)

Education

(1) Bachelor of Science
Food Technology
East Memphis University, 1980

(2) Certified Food Technologist (CFT)
1983

(3) **Overview:** Nine years of progressively more responsible food processing industry positions involving both production and research and development.

(4) Capabilities

(5) • Experienced in FDA-based texture and temperature testing technology as it applies to juice, convenience meals, and bulk vegetable preparation.

• Supervision of processing personnel and team leaders — native language capabilities in Spanish. (6)

(7) • Participation in sales, advertising, and marketing research — included regular consultation with ad agency personnel regarding verifiable claims of nutritional content and taste validity.

Achievements

(8) • Recipient of the 1987 Golden Platter Award from the convenience food marketing association for excellence in technical support consultation.

• Top bonus award 1984 earned for equipment selection recommendations that resulted in savings of $138,000 over previous year's operations due to 24 percent reduction in contract staff maintenance costs.

(9) • Member of a three person team credited with the 1988 discovery of the frozen gravy stabilization technique (FGST) now the standard of the convenience food industry.

Employment

(10) November 1987 - Present: Food Chemist, Dinner Time Frozen Foods, Memphis, TN.

January 1983 - October 1987: Production Supervisor, Minuterite Natural Juices, Inc., Ocala, FL.

July 1980 - December 1982: Junior Food Chemist, King of Vegetables Processors, Salinas, CA.

35. Fund Raiser

FOCUSED RESUME

General Strategy

Mr. Oden is a private fund raiser for private colleges. He uses a resume to make his services known and to present his firm for consideration as the institutions select those who will assist them in the coming year. His employment record is relevant, but this specialized need is best met by the **Focused Resume.**

The resume will focus attention on:

- his own prestigious college background;

- the style of his work, as much as its substance; and

- respectability by association.

Specific Points

① The Yale degree constitutes instant endorsement for his work and is featured prominently as is his most appropriate major in marketing.

② **Summary** says what he does, with whom, and for how long.

③ Dollars and cents results couched in tasteful terms.

④ The promise of a commercial quality campaign that won't look that way.

⑤ Clients identify and classify the practitioner in this business.

⑥ Employment history is given a classier name with the implication that he has been more than a mere employee.

⑦ His own firm is identified—little description needed here since the whole resume is focused on defining that image.

⑧ A campus development (fund raising) position adds to credibility.

⑨ Five years in big-time advertising circles brings commercial respectability.

⑩ The solicitation itself is tastefully and briefly held for last. Cover letter also amplifies the purpose of this communication—to seek additional clients.

Ronald P. Oden

43 Aiken Avenue
Charleston, SC 29403
803-222-9988 (Office)
803-333-9075 (Residence)

Education

Bachelor of Science
Marketing
Yale University, 1974

Summary: Experienced marketing professional with 6 years of outstanding performance as an institutional fund raiser in the private college sector.

Performance Characteristics

- Ambitiously realistic goal setting with institutional leaders and mentors.

- Alumni participation rates consistently exceed industry standards by 25 percent or more.

- Noted for tastefully conducted, professional campaign with the impact of a commercial promotion, the feel of a traditional appeal.

- Goals consistently exceeded by an average of 15 percent.

Current Client List

Alverno College, Texas

Asbury College, Maine

Bard University, New Mexico

Defiant College, Kentucky

Hope University, South Carolina

Rockhurst Academy, Michigan

Sacred Dominican University, Indiana

Whitman College, California

Present and Prior Affiliations

1983 - Present: President and Chief Executive Officer, Ronald P. Oden and Associates, Ltd., Charleston, SC. Consultants to the annual giving and special project financing of private institutions of higher education nationally.

1980 - 1983: Director of Development, Witherspoon College, NH.

1975 - 1980: Associate, The John Melon Krumpright Agency, New York, NY.

Comments: Currently accepting invitations for proposals for the 1991-92 college giving year. I would welcome the opportunity to consider your needs.

36. Graphic Designer

COMPETENCY CLUSTER RESUME

General Strategy

Ms. Lyle is a graphic artist with a continuous work history, but she is more interested in establishing an array of special competencies. The way to do that is to use the **Competency Cluster Resume** in which the skills gained in several settings are pulled together and presented as one.

This resume will be directed toward:

- identifying her as a technologically up-to-the-minute artist;

- establishing her solid foundation in traditional settings; and

- pulling it all together around the right awards, credentials, and past affiliations.

Specific Points

1. Since she has the equipment and graphic art is her field, a modest amount of style is added to the resume with lines and unusual type faces.

2. **Competencies** establishes her three main skill areas.

3. Computer graphics is highlighted, since it is a highly marketable specialty.

4. Enough technical jargon is used to communicate understanding.

5. No computer-capable graphic artist would be complete without desktop publishing credentials, so they are established.

6. Confirmation that all the technology is underwritten by the skills of a basic artist.

7. Awards selected to show across-the-board excellence.

8. Employment history is continuous and correct.

9. Her degree is the right one and from a respected institution.

10. **Comments** clarifies what she is out to accomplish with her career move.

Patricia D. Lyle
51-C Mount Pleasant Drive
Providence, RI 02908
401-222-9988 (Office)
401-333-9075 (Residence)

○ Competencies ○

Computer Graphics

Color and B&W graphics capabilities using Aldus Freehand on the Macintosh II computer system. Experienced in using both text and graphic scanners. Preparation of products at 300 dpi and full professional quality formats. Expert at trace modification art and logo design.

Desktop Publishing

Oversized Radius screen used for layout of single illustration and multipage publications with desktop publishing software, principally PageMaker. Experienced in brochure, tabloid, magazine, and newspaper layout — expert integration of graphics, including photography.

Drawing Board Artist

Nine years of combined college and commercial experience. Began as illustrator and paste-up person for university publications. Followed by three years of newspaper and two years of national magazine advertising and story art.

○ Awards ○

- Computer Monthly Magazine, 1989 First Place Award for Commercial Graphics
- The New England Gazette Syndicate, 1985 Award for Excellence in Advertising Graphics
- Numerous collegiate graphic arts and journalism awards

○ Employment ○

1987 - Date: Senior Graphic Artist, Rhode Island Weekends Magazine, Providence, RI.

1985 - 1987: Paste-up and Insertion Technician, The Providence Daily, Providence, RI.

1983 - 1985: Free-Lance Artist/Photographer

○ Education ○

Bachelor of Arts
Commercial Design
Rhode Island College of Design, 1983

○ Comments ○

Interested in taking combined artistic, journalistic, and commercial experience and applying it in a computer-equipped graphic arts studio.

37. Heating, Air Conditioning, and Refrigeration Mechanic

FOCUSED RESUME

General Strategy

Mr. Blackwell is a recent technical graduate who needs to emphasize his strengths independent of a traditional employment listing. His best choice is the **Focused Resume,** which will allow him to:

- highlight his excellent technical education;
- show that he has had significant work experience, if not regular jobs; and
- indicate that he has excelled in several categories that have relevance for occupational success.

Specific Points

1. The right degree for his specialty from a respected local junior college.

2. **Introduction** establishes him as a properly prepared recent graduate with references ready to vouch for his potential.

3. In the absence of a full-time work history, the resume properly focuses on academic preparation, experience related to training, and evidence of excellence—awards.

4. In his urban market, the specialized skills can be attractive to a large firm.

5. Summer work with a respected firm adds credibility and potential references.

6. Evidence of ability to deal with older equipment as well as the most modern.

7. Work-study experience provided experience and showed initiative.

8. Quantification of the situation helps others judge its relevance to them.

9. Awards provide unbiased endorsement of excellence and promise.

10. Note shows awareness of the next steps to take professionally and the fact that they are being actively pursued.

Harold S. Blackwell
45 Cheney Creek Road
Philadelphia, PA 19153
215-333-9075

Education

(1)

Associate in Applied Science
Heating, Air-Conditioning, and Refrigeration Technology
Philadelphia Junior College, 1989

(2) **Introduction:** Recent graduate with up-to-the-minute technical training and work-study experiences with latest commercial and institutional cooling and heating units. Excellent trade and academic references available. Seek growth opportunity in my field.

Academic Preparation

- Completed a two-year, 90 quarter hour, Heating & Cooling Institute accredited course of study concentrating on commercial and institutional installations.
- (4) Specializations included plant failure diagnostics, passive heat loss control, and third generation heat pump installation and maintenance.

Work Experience

(3)

- (5) Two summers of full-time employment with Jones & Whitman Engineering, Inc., installing new heating and air-conditioning plants in commercial buildings. Last three weeks of each summer spent servicing, in preparation for the heating season, existing heating systems ranging in age from new to 20 years. ← (6)
- 17 hours weekly college work-study experience with the maintenance department of (7) Philadelphia Junior College District. Assisted in the maintenance of 4 separate heating, air-conditioning and refrigeration systems serving (8) the 327,000 square foot facility.

Awards

- (9) Quail Industries Student Trouble-Shooter of the Year Award for 1989, presented at their annual meeting in Washington, DC.
- Honors Graduate, Philadelphia Junior College, Technical Division, 1989

Note: Currently pursuing National Association of Heating, Air-Conditioning, and Refrigeration Technicians' professional certification. Anticipate having the Certified NAHACRT designation in minimum time following three years of qualifying full-time work experience and supervision. (10)

38. Hospital Administrator

WORK HISTORY RESUME

General Strategy

Ms. Munford has held only two full-time positions, but they are sufficiently well defined to describe her capabilities and accomplishments. She has selected the **Work History Resume** in order to show:

- the right degrees for a career in hospital administration;

- solid, successful experience in the number-two slot at a major hospital; and

- prior experience that adds to her credibility in managing resources.

Specific Points

① The undergraduate degree in Business Administration would be adequate.

② Add a master's degree in Hospital Administration and you have a combination worthy of leading the resume.

③ **Overview** tells the reviewer what is to come and the presenter's objective.

④ **Employment History** is brief, but totally relevant—also accounts for all dates.

⑤ Position is clarified beyond title to show full responsibilities.

⑥ The institution is described to convey the scope of what she manages.

⑦ Strength in hospital personnel management is verified.

⑧ Familiarity with hospital accreditation is noted.

⑨ Since it is highly relevant, military experience is detailed.

⑩ Commendation for excellent performance is worth noting.

Dea S. Munford
84 Newburg Avenue
Eugene, OR 97405
503-222-9988 (Office)
503-333-9075 (Residence)

Education

① Bachelor of Science
Business Administration
Smithson University, Oregon 1979

② Master of Science
Hospital Administration
Oregon State University 1984

③ Overview: Experienced administrative officer with nearly ten years of institutional finance and personnel management experience, 5 of them in a hospital setting. Desires to assume chief hospital administrator position in a mid-size urban institution.

④ Employment History

1984 - Date: *Assistant General Administrator*, Eugene Memorial Hospital, Eugene, OR. • Second ranking administrative officer in a 375 bed, **⑤** 84 doctor general care facility serving a suburban population of **⑥** 123,000 residents. • Manage a budget of $22 million dollars **⑦** annually. • Responsible for staff liaison and labor contracting. • Major role in rate negotiations with insurance carriers. • Designated coordinator of combined annual giving and community volunteer program. •Achieved outstanding results in all areas including: 38 percent reduction in nursing staff turnover, contracts maintained within CPI guidelines, and hospital restored to full accreditation after 2 years of probation. **⑧**

1983 - 1984: Full-time graduate study.

1979 - 1983: *Personnel and Finance Officer*, United States Navy, Norfolk and **⑨** San Diego. • Officer in charge of personnel and financial records management for carrier squadrons 9 and 37 out of the ports of Norfolk and San Diego. • Accountable to senior managers and commanders for a bi-weekly payroll of $678,000 dollars. • All personnel records maintained according to Navy regulations. • **⑩** Navy Commendation Medal awarded upon change of command and return to inactive reserve status.

39. Hotel Manager

WORK HISTORY RESUME

General Strategy

Mr. Brown has pursued the expected career ladder and each position provides a forum for his accomplishments at that level. His choice of the **Work History Resume** is a correct one.

The resume will be structured to show:

- a degree directly related to the job pursued;

- a career path that moves logically from entry level to management; and

- an explanation of why he wants to make a career move now.

Specific Points

① Hotel Management degree from Cornell is worth featuring.

② **Introduction** notes length and level of service in the industry.

③ **Experience** is a textbook example of upward mobility in the hospitality industry.

④ Clarification of reporting authority within the organization and the nature of the property managed are both important in establishing his level.

⑤ Verifiable measure of excellence noted.

⑥ Quantified depiction of the property and his role in its management are needed.

⑦ Success in managing a specialized profit center is worthy of note.

⑧ Valuable to demonstrate success in a turn-around situation—even at this less-than-comprehensive management level.

⑨ States what it would take to entice him to move on.

⑩ Shows that he is continuing to build his industry credentials.

Darrell T. Brown

763 Boone Street, NW
Norman, OK 73070
405-222-9988 (Office)
405-333-9075 (Residence)

Education

Bachelor of Science
Hotel Management
 Cornell University, 1981

 Introduction: Nine years of successful experience in positions of growing management responsibility in commercial chain hotels catering to up-scale business travelers in the continental United States.

 Experience

1987 - Present

 Manager, Hildome Resident Business Suites, Norman, OK. Site Manager responsible to a Regional Manager for the complete operation of a 214 unit suites-only business travel facility near the university research park. Supervise a food and beverage manager and housekeeping manager in addition to contract grounds maintenance services and security. Led the region past 3 quarters in ratio analysis profitability.

1984 - 1987

Assistant Manager, Airport Inns of America, O'Hare International Airport, Chicago, IL. Reported to the General Manager while serving as the second in charge of the total management of this 387 room middle market business traveler's airport hotel. Special duties included group and ⑦ convention sales staff supervision. An area in which O'Hare achieved a 500 percent increase in bookings during my tenure.

1981 - 1984

Food and Beverage Manager, Lakeside Inn and Conference Center, Avalon Lake, NY. Assumed management of a failing restaurant, conference, and room service operation in this 277 ⑧ room business resort facility and turned it into a profit center in 17 months. Converted kitchen from traditional preparation to local chef's entree supplemented by top quality prepared supporting products. Reduced staff by 65 percent, reinvested proceeds in upgrading chef and investing in state-of-the-art high intensity cooking facilities.

⑨ **Comments:** Reason for leaving — To pursue multiple unit, regional management responsibilities with a major national business property. Continuing Education — Enrolled in the final section of the Hotel Managers Institute remote learning series leading to designation as a Certified Hotel General Manager (CHGM). Completion expected next summer. ⑩

40. Insurance Agent

WORK HISTORY RESUME

General Strategy

Mr. McClay has moved successfully and profitably up the insurance sales career ladder. The jobs he has held are perfect devices for displaying his talents and the nature of his accomplishments. He is well advised to present himself on the strength of his professional positions arrayed in a standard **Work History Resume.**

His resume will be used to:

- show a logical insurance career path;
- classify himself as a successful group sales agent; and
- state his objective of achieving participating status in an agency.

Specific Points

1. **Overview** is used to identify his segment of the industry.
2. His objective of becoming a business partner in an agency is also noted up front.
3. Experience is arrayed to show movement in timely fashion from individual sales to major group sales.
4. His present position is described in the terms of the industry.
5. Ability to train and manage other agents is an attractive partner quality.
6. Results that can be shown in profit-generating numbers are impressive.
7. Another successful group sales situation is described quantitatively.
8. Clients and products are described and measures of success noted.
9. Power as a one-on-one salesman is always worth establishing, as are the basic certifications of the industry and the fact that they have been achieved.
10. The college degree is a basic credential worth noting—nothing to stress.

Robert J. McClay

12-F Devils Lake Avenue
Columbus, OH 43209
614-222-9988 (Office)
614-333-9075 (Residence)

(1) **Overview:** Twelve years of successful group sales with life and health products of a single underwriter in the institutional non-profit segment of the market. Seeking partnership interest in an agency engaged in these aspects of insurance marketing. *(2)*

Experience

(4)

June 1987 - Present: *Senior Group Sales Agent*, The Haas Agency, Suite 300, Embassy Square, Columbus, OH. Manager in charge of 4 salespersons concentrating on the colleges in North Central Ohio and *(5)* Western Pennsylvania. Duties include training and motivation for ←*(5)* those under my supervision and sales presentations to principal client institutions. 1989 revenues for my segment exceeded 1988 by 300 percent. New accounts added in 37 colleges and universities *(6)* previously serviced by national firms.

(3) June 1983 - May 1987: *Group Sales Representative*, Wilcox & Wilson Insurance Agency, Inc., One South River Front Road, Columbus, OH. Lead group sales representative for the number one volume firm for *(7)* non-profits in Columbus. Served hospitals, professional organizations, and governmental entities within a 50 mile radius of Columbus with life and health packages. Multi-Million Dollar Roundtable member *(8)* 1984 through 1987, logging higher combined sales than all but 17 other similarly situated agents in the Eastern United States.

July 1977 - May 1983: *Agent*, Ohio Life and Casualty, Cleveland, OH. *(9)* Sale of individual life and casualty products to professional clients in the greater Cleveland market. Exceeded company production records for a new hire agent in 13 months and opted to enter their group sales division where I remained until 1983, learned the business and earned all relevant professional licenses, certifications, and designations.

Education

(10) Bachelor of Arts
Liberal Arts
Clarkson University, Pennsylvania, 1977

41. Interior Designer

FOCUSED RESUME

General Strategy

Mr. Gilbert has done some things that make him attractive as a decorator and they are best viewed when pulled together from their separate occupational experience sources. To do this he has correctly selected the **Focused Resume** format.

His resume will have the objective of *focusing* the reviewer's attention on those several qualities and experiences that constitute his main assets:

- academic credentials appropriate to his field;
- urban experience; and
- commercially successful accomplishments in various settings.

Specific Points

1. A traditional college program in the arts is offered as a basic credential.

2. Specialized training in a recognized design institution adds an important dimension.

3. **Strengths** all cater to the large urban market to which he again aspires.

4. Points out the power combination of training he possesses.

5. Experience is confirmed in accepted settings and situations.

6. **Accomplishments** show that he is commercially successful.

7. Versatility is evidenced in a range of projects that reach from an institutional setting to a piece of commercial equipment to a prestigious home.

8. Magazine article recognition is important endorsement.

9. Work chronology is necessary, but requires no elaboration beyond that given above.

10. **Comments** describe desire to return to urban market.

Thomas K. Gilbert
32 Bismark Drive, NW
Minot, ND 58701
701-222-9988 (Office)
701-333-9075 (Residence)

Goal: To obtain a decorator's position with an established urban interior design studio.

Education

 Bachelor of Arts
Art History
Smith University, 1983

 Certificate
Interior Design
New York School of Design, 1987

 ### Strengths

 • Educated in the classic art tradition, yet specifically trained in the practical aspects of the contemporary design industry.

• Two years of full-time experience with the commercial design firm of Winston Interiors, Ltd., New York.

• One year of teaching and working as a free-lance interior designer with residential clients in an urban setting.

• Three years of part-time commercial design work on referral basis while a full-time student at the New York School of Design.

Accomplishments

• Redesigned the Minot Air Force Base Officers Club which subsequently won the 1989 Strategic Air Command Award for Non-Appropriated Funds Facilities Improvement.

• Credited with the selection of colors and textures used in the bulkhead tapestries for the new Trunpet Shuttle 727D airliners while a Winston Associate in 1988.

• Residential design of the William S. Peed apartment in New York, done on a free-lance basis while a student, featured in NY Apartment Living Magazine, June 1984.

Chronology

<u>1988 - Present</u>: Self-employed interior designer, Minot, ND.

<u>1987 - 1988</u>: Commercial Design Associate, Winston Interiors, Ltd., New York.

<u>1984 - 1987</u>: Full-time student in interior design, New York.

<u>1983 - 1984</u>: Teacher of Art History, Darien Saints Preparatory School, Darien, CT.

Comments: After returning to small town environment and opening my own studio, am convinced that the best opportunity to reach my potential is in the city.

42. Landscape Architect

WORK HISTORY RESUME

General Strategy

Ms. McGee has a very straightforward presentation to make that involves two periods of employment that directly represent her skills and interests. For that objective, nothing is better suited than the **Work History Resume.**

She will rely on her resume to:

- communicate her basic education and experience; and

- recount specific projects that speak to her ability to handle both the technical and public relations work associated with the position she seeks.

Specific Points

1. Landscape architecture is the ideal degree and worthy of prominence in this brief resume.

2. The **Objective** is used to identify a specific position for which she is applying.

3. **Experience** is brief and pointed since it is directed toward a specific objective.

4. Present position title endorses her as a player in the local restoration community.

5. Her public position will not be that different from the proposed foundation position she seeks, so the comparison is appropriate.

6. Many of the duties will be essentially the same in both jobs.

7. Experience obtaining grant money is going to be an attractive quality.

8. Commercial developers will be involved in the Lowlands project and this shows she is familiar with how they work.

9. Specific roles in community development will be valuable.

10. Ability to work with community and government groups will be essential, so it is worth providing evidence that she can do this.

Wanda H. McGee

87 New Bern Road
Greenville, NC 27858
919-222-9988 (Office)
919-333-9075 (Residence)

Education

(1) Bachelor of Science
Landscape Architecture
South Carolina University, 1983

(2) **Objective:** Applying for the position of Landscape Architect II with the Historic Lowlands Foundation, Charleston, SC.

(3) Experience

(5) May 1986 - Present: *Resident Landscape Architect* (4)
Old Town Historical Society, Greenville, SC.

(6)
- Report to the City Manager and responsible for the design and management of public green spaces within Greenville.
- Close working relationship with Park Authority, Department of Highways, and other agencies impacting the green spaces.
- Coordinated park restoration project which involved excavation and re-establishment of an historic garden in downtown district.
- Provided technical and cost estimate support for local resident drive to save the vintage peach trees lining Woodrow Marsh Avenue in suburban Greenville.
- Secured federal grant for the study of requirements and funding needed for the restoration of Meeting Square Gardens, private residential plots (7) adjoining the town square.

(9) June 1983 - April 1986: *Architectural Design Assistant-Exterior* (8)
Bantum Development Company, Atlanta, GA.

- Layout and specifications designer for major developer in the greater Atlanta area.
- Reported to the Chief Landscape Architect and responded to requests for assistance with land treatments beyond the walls of project structures.
- Liaison with community and government environmental and preservation groups. (10)

43. Legal Assistant

COMPETENCY CLUSTER RESUME

General Strategy

Ms. DeMagio has an acceptable, but undistinguished work history. It will make a stronger presentation if her competencies are extracted and showcased instead of her jobs. To do that she will use the **Competency Cluster Resume.**

In making the most of her skills, she will use her resume to:

- show that she can prepare all sorts of materials for legal cases; and

- demonstrate that she can prepare individual and corporate legal documents.

Specific Points

(1) The starting point for her paralegal resume is an associate degree in the field.

(2) **Competencies** constitutes a three-item summary with supporting detail.

(3) All of the basic skills of paralegal case preparation are acknowledged here.

(4) Affidavit taking can constitute a specialty in its own right.

(5) Document preparation is a mainstay of the paralegal, so it is supported here.

(6) Depending on the concentration of the hiring firm, it may be more important to have corporate skills, so they are developed separately.

(7) The employment history shows steady, relevant employment.

(8) Both corporate and institutional experience are available, so they are cited.

(9) Private-practice experience still represents a large segment of the potential employers, so it is covered separately.

(10) Professionalism is shown by the appropriate affiliations.

Joanne G. DeMagio
7-B Flushing Drive
Plattsburg, NY 12903
518-222-9988 (Office)
518-333-9075 (Residence)

Education

① Associate in Science
Paralegal Technology
Junior College of Staten Island, 1983

Competencies

Case Preparation
• Background work for cases pending before the courts.
③ • Researched appropriate laws, judicial decisions and drafted written opinions.
• Prepared preliminary arguments and pleadings.
• Obtained affidavits. ←④

②

Document Preparation
⑤
• Prepared draft contracts, mortgages, separation agreements, tax returns, estate and trust instruments.

Corporate Support
⑥
• Assisted in preparing employment applications, contracts, shareholder agreements, employee benefit plans, loan documents, and annual financial reports.

Employment History

June 1987 - Present: Legal Assistant, The Kilgore Corporation, Plattsburg, NY.
⑧

⑦ June 1983 - May 1987: Legal Aide, Trust Company of Northwest New York, Irvington, NY.

May 1983 - December 1984: Legal Technician, Joseph, Joseph, and Wilkins, Attorneys at Law, Ithaca, NY.
⑨

Professional Memberships

National Association of Legal Assistants
State Bar Association, Legal Assistants Division
⑩

44. Library Technician

COMPETENCY CLUSTER RESUME

General Strategy

Mr. Warden is a recent liberal arts graduate at the associate degree level. His challenge is to portray himself as what he legitimately is—a rather well-trained library technician. With neither the degree title or full-time work experience to support his claim, he is well advised to present himself in the context of a **Competency Cluster Resume** that can:

- highlight his various less-than-formal, but valuable library experiences; and

- explain that his degree is more than it appears to be.

Specific Points

(1) With no full-time position, it would be inappropriate to list an office phone.

(2) Experience is arranged in such a manner as to show two strong clusters of highly relevant library experience.

(3) One dimension is the technical services area addressed here.

(4) Specific experience includes the latest technology—CD/ROM disk.

(5) Experienced in the clerical aspects of library work.

(6) Further evidence of involvement with library technology.

(7) The second major cluster is user services, developed here.

(8) Examples include both front desk and telephone work assisting the public.

(9) Degree is noted and clarified effectively with verification offered.

(10) Professional affiliation is useful even at the entry level.

Barry W. Warden

98 Levermour Street
Las Cruces, NM 88004
505-333-9075 (Residence)

② Experience

TECHNICAL SERVICES

- Assisted faculty and students in the use of the library's newly installed CD/ROM databases for card catalog, periodicals and newspapers.

- Prepared documents for shipment to microfilm copying service.

- Validated information requests for technical research.

- Participated in the conversion of library catalog holdings to electronic media.

USER SERVICES ⑦

- Manned New Mexico Library Consortium Hotline as a volunteer responding to statewide inquiries about library use and resources.

- Work-study desk clerk 20 hours per week at the college library for two years of full-time study.

Education

Associate in Arts
Portales Community College, 1989

Comments

Degree in library technology not approved at Portales Community College, but took a concentration of 15 semester hours in related courses. See college transcript for verification and specifics.

⑩ Professional Affiliation

Associate Member: American Library Association

45. Manufacturers' Sales Representative

COMPETENCY CLUSTER RESUME

General Strategy

Ms. Black is an engineer and a salesperson. Her objective is to convey both technical competency and the ability to sell this class of products and services. Since only one of her three positions deals with sales, she has correctly elected to present herself in the framework of the **Competency Cluster Resume.**

Her use of the resume is to:

- demonstrate field sales competency with technical clients;

- show familiarity with the field and manufacturing aspects of her product line; and

- establish credibility as as serious sales professional.

Specific Points

1. Since she is seeking a sales rep position, her address may have some relevance—in this case it is a good jumping-off point for working her desired territory.

2. Overview tells the story of her dual experiences and her objective of joining an appropriate manufacturers' rep agency.

3. **Competencies** is used as a heading to highlight her three areas of greatest strength.

4. Technical selling is the lead item since it points directly to what she seeks.

5. Knowledge of codes, estimating, and field sales support technology are rightly stressed.

6. This item establishes that she can relate to customers—she's been there.

7. She knows the product line from the manufacturing perspective—strong selling point in the field.

8. Employment history covers all that is necessary to say—emphasis has already been placed earlier in the resume.

9. Appropriate technical degree noted.

10. Affiliations reflect commitment to professional sales career.

Frances C. Black
2-A Cinnaminson Road
Hackettstown, NJ 07840
201-222-9988 (Office)
201-333-9075 (Residence)

Overview: More than 6 years of combined civil engineering experience in the manufacturer, contractor, and sales representative sectors. Seeking an expanded manufacturers' representative opportunity in association with an established agency.

Competencies

<u>TECHNICAL SALES</u>

- Market a full line of heavy drainage and conduit products to contractors in the New York, New Jersey, and Eastern Pennsylvania region.
- Experienced estimator familiar with various codes and ordinances as well as the product line.
- Accomplished user of the laptop computer for on-site demonstrations and estimates and remote order placement and field support communications via modem.

<u>FIELD ENGINEER</u>

- Supervision of survey and design crews in the construction of interstate highway systems.
- Specifications engineer for the district office of a state highway department with field verification responsibilities.

<u>MANUFACTURING</u>

- Design and testing of pre-cast concrete components for highway drainage systems.
- Familiarity with the materials and manufacturing processes involved in producing pre-cast civil engineering components.

Employment History

<u>November 1988 - Present</u>: Manufacturers Representative, Norton & Associates, Inc., Denville, NJ. One of three independent contractor sales representatives coordinated by the Norton agency.

<u>April 1985 - October 1988</u>: Field Engineer, New Jersey Department of Highways, Dover District Office, Dover, NJ.

<u>August 1983 - March 1985</u>: Staff Civil Engineer, Concrete Castings, Ltd., Edison, NJ. Design and testing for largest manufacturer of pre-cast drainage system components in New Jersey.

Education

Bachelor of Science
Civil Engineering
Fairleigh Dickinson University, 1983

Trade Affiliations

Women in Sales
Manufacturers Agents National Association

46. Medical-Records Technician

FOCUSED RESUME

General Strategy

Mr. Webb has three jobs, all in his field of Medical-Records Technology, but they amount to an unfocused summary of his true capabilities and achievements. When he put it all together in a **Focused Resume,** here is what he was able to accentuate:

- the right degree and professional certification;

- an aggregate of valuable experience and a goal to match; and

- a clearly presented set of capabilities and achievements.

Specific Points

(1) The associate degree in his specialty leads his resume.

(2) Professional certification follows.

(3) **Overview** provides a focus in summary form and states the occupational objective.

(4) The size facility is important for the position sought, so it is prominently mentioned.

(5) **Capabilities** are shown in the terms recognized and valued by those who would review his resume.

(6) A mix of technical and supervisory tasks supports aspiration to management.

(7) **Achievements** are phrased to show bottom-line consciousness.

(8) They demonstate effectiveness in hospital and **HMO** environments.

(9) Employment is listed matter-of-factly after emphasis was placed earlier in the resume.

(10) Range of experience from insurance company to hospital and **HMO** gives widest possible job market potential for his skills.

Kenneth N. Webb
78 Portsmouth Street
Manchester, NH 03103
603-222-9988 (Office)
603-333-9075 (Residence)

EDUCATION

① → Associate in Applied Science
Medical Records Technology
New Hampshire Community College, 1983

② → Accredited Records Technician (ART)
American Medical Record Association

③ **OVERVIEW:** Six years of increasingly responsible positions in the medical records field with in-depth exposure to hospital, insurance, and health management organization systems. Seek a supervisory medical records administrator position in a 500 bed or larger care facility.

④ ↗ ## CAPABILITIES

- Code and record diseases, operations, and therapeutic procedures according to standard classification systems.
- Oversee the accurate transcription of medical records by clerks.
⑤ - Conduct analyses of patient medical records for reporting and statistical purposes. ⑥
- Quality control of medical records for completeness, consistency, and accuracy.

ACHIEVEMENTS

- Completed the conversion of 35 years accumulated insurance medical records to modern computer coding and microform.
⑦ - Devised major hospital governmental reporting procedures that satisfied regulatory requirements and reduced staff time involved by 31 percent. ⑧
- Implemented a records clerk training program at the HMO that speeded entry by 48 percent and reduced errors by 82 percent.

EMPLOYMENT

June 1987 - Present: Medical Records Technician, Old New Hampshire Life
⑨ and Casualty Company, Manchester, NH.

December 1985 - May 1987: Medical Records Technician, Boston Health ⑩
Management Organization, Boston, MA.

June 1983 - November 1985: Coding and Recording Technician,
Northeastern Community Hospital, Bayside, NH.

47. Minister

FOCUSED RESUME

General Strategy

Mr. Chapman is a minister and the expectation is that one position will look pretty much like the last. He needs a device for bringing out the special strengths that he has developed in this series of similar positions—the **Focused Resume** is the preferred format to accomplish his goal.

The minister's resume will assist him in:

- demonstrating such things as his affinity for working with the business community;

- showing his expertise in church physical plant management; and

- making the point that he is effective in setting and achieving major goals.

Specific Points

1. **Strengths** show a series of special skills that might be lost or stated repetitiously in a more traditional resume format.

2. Since businesspersons often sit on church boards and selection committees, his mention of being able to work with them successfully is germane.

3. An ability to communicate effectively beyond the pulpit is cited here.

4. **Achievements** as a topic gives him a forum for mentioning goals set and met.

5. The results of his businesslike approach are given in human terms meaningful to the congregation.

6. Leadership and the ability to take initiatives that work and are worthy of replication by others is shown in this point.

7. Specific, tangible achievements are noted.

8. A proper career progression stands alone, with the exceptional aspects already noted.

9. A respectable undergraduate degree is confirmed.

10. Ordination is also shown, since it is the ultimate arbiter of his eligibility.

Harold J. Chapman

89 Atlantic Drive
Omaha, NE 68102
402-222-9988 (Office)
402-333-9075 (Residence)

Goal: To lead the congregation of a new church
in a growing suburban setting.

Strengths

- Heavily involved in regional activities with particular attention to involving the secular business community in positive social commitments.
- Particularly knowledgeable of church physical plant management.
- Committed to staff development, especially involving clergy-in-training and the church youth activities systems.
- Popular articles published in religious and secular journals.

Achievements

- Increased business community giving by 67 percent over a two year period in current assignment.
- Lowered operating costs by 23 percent by implementing a physical plant modernization campaign that involved contributed labor and materials.
- Initiated the House The Poor Foundation in 1984 that has grown to a system now used throughout the Western Region.
- Encouraged a parishioner-based fund drive that yielded core investment for sanctuary elevator and air-conditioning that resulted in improved retention of active elderly members.

Experience

June 1987 - Present: Minister, Main Street Methodist Church, Omaha, NE.

June 1983 - May 1987: Minister, Asbury Methodist Church, Pueblo, CO.

July 1979 - May 1983: Associate Minister, First Street United Methodist Church, Las Vegas, NV.

Education

Bachelor of Arts
English Literature
Nevada University
1977

Ordination
Methodist Minister
Columbia Southern Seminary
1979

48. Newspaper Reporter

COMPETENCY CLUSTER RESUME

General Strategy

Ms. O'Hare is in a field that lends itself well to identifying specific, valuable groups of professional skills. While they are not totally lost in a traditional job listing resume, they can be emphasized quite effectively in a **Competency Cluster Resume.**

Her resume is crafted to show:

- four very specific areas of competency;
- enough detail to give them meaning; and
- confirmation of a suitable career path for the position sought.

Specific Points

① A journalism degree is central to a reporter's career, so it is the lead item.

② Four skill areas form the most obvious heart of her resume and communicate a great deal even without the associated elaboration.

③ Emphasis is placed on the skill most relevant to her career aspiration.

④ The numbers show a potential syndicator that she has serious potential.

⑤ Nuts and bolts reporting skills are confirmed here.

⑥ Evidence of initiative and courage that could spark a winning column.

⑦ Four years in the big time add credibility to her desire to address national issues.

⑧ **Employment** record shows a plausible rise through the ranks.

⑨ Affiliations add to professional image.

⑩ Comments indicate what she seeks—expanded on in her cover letter.

Susan T. O'Hare
5 North Harvey Street
Great Falls, MT 59405
406-232-9988 (Office)
406-323-9075 (Residence)

Education

①

Bachelor of Science
Journalism
Southern Montana University, 1981

Competencies

FEATURE WRITING
③

Writer of a regionally syndicated
feature on environmental and sport
fishing concerns. Readership
estimated at 350,000; subscribers ④
increasing 22 percent annually.

CITY REPORTING

②

Two years as a city desk reporter
covering court, jail, and
⑤ community activities for an urban
population of 140,000.

INVESTIGATIVE REPORTING

Developed sources and published
stories that led to the indictment ⑥
of the mayor on drug charges.

CORRESPONDENT REPORTING

Four years representing second
largest paper in the state in ⑦
Washington, DC.

Employment

June 1987 - Present: Feature Writer, Great Falls Courier, Great Falls,
MT.

⑧ January 1983 - May 1987: Correspondent, The Minnesota Times Service,
Washington, DC.

July 1981 - December 1983: City Reporter, Minnesota Evening Times,
Duluth, MN.

⑨ ### Professional Affiliations

Women in Communications
North Central Print Journalists' Guild

Comments: Seeking an upper Mid-West newspaper affiliation from which
to develop a syndicated column.

⑩

49. Nurse

COMPETENCY CLUSTER RESUME

General Strategy

Ms. Purcell is a nurse with special skills to emphasize. She will use the **Competency Cluster Resume** in order to make her point.

Her resume is designed in such a manner as to:

- highlight her three strongest areas of competency;

- reinforce the skill areas by providing meaningful specifics; and

- show her educational progression and the goal it is intended to achieve.

Specific Points

(1) **Overview** makes the major point of the resume—experienced associate degree nurse about to become bachelor's degree nurse and assume greater responsibility.

(2) **Competencies** make the case for her comprehensive experience—key words known in the profession take on an almost graphic quality in this format.

(3) Types the hospital and kinds of services in a way that will be understood.

(4) Places herself within a nationally known rating scheme.

(5) Specialized experience is emphasized here.

(6) Supervision experience is noted—relevant to aspirations.

(7) Another care dimension added with part-time experience.

(8) **Employment History** backs what she has claimed elsewhere in the resume.

(9) Her basic associate degree in nursing is noted.

(10) The expected completion date is listed as a proper qualifier on the bachelor's degree.

Delores K. Purcell, R.N.
3 Cook Avenue, Apartment 172
Columbia, MO 65203
314-222-9988 (Office)
314-333-9075 (Residence)

(1) **Overview:** Associate degree registered nurse with 6 years of full-time professional experience nearing completion of bachelor's degree seeking supervisory or nurse practitioner opportunity.

Competencies

(2) • GENERAL NURSING — Floor nurse in two major hospitals (500 bed facilities) with comprehensive care responsibilities including assisting physicians, (3) providing treatment, and the administration of medications, physical examinations, and inoculations. Have attained level 4 on the 5-level career-ladder of experienced professional nurses. (4)

• POSTOPERATIVE CARE — Implement physician prescribed treatment (5) regimens for patients recovering from surgery. Special training in resuscitation assistance for cardiac patients. Experienced in the supervision of L.P.N. services in the postoperative-care environment. (6)

• CONVALESCENT CARE — Weekend duty at a convalescent home caring for 274 elderly convalescents provided experience in this sector. Familiar (7) with the treatment regimens and recurring problems found in this population.

Employment History

(8) September 1985 - Present: Postoperative-Care Nurse, Our Lady of Hope Hospital, Columbia, MO.

May 1983 - August 1985: Staff Nurse, Central Memorial Hospital, Springfield, MO.

Education

Associate of Science
Nursing
Central Community College, MO
1983
(9)

Bachelor of Science
Clinical Nursing
North Central Missouri University
(June graduation anticipated)
(10)

50. Personnel Specialist

COMPETENCY CLUSTER RESUME

General Strategy

Ms. Stuart wants to structure her resume in such a way as to place an emphasis on the competencies most highly valued in her profession. She has a long work history that relates well to her career objectives, but the position-by-position style resume tends to obscure the points she wants to make. The solution is the **Competency Cluster Resume** that will allow her to:

- showcase her special groups of skills;
- provide the specifics needed to make them meaningful; and
- back it all with a logical progression of positions held.

Specific Points

① With a private office, a discreet call to her business phone presents no problem, so it can be listed along with the home phone.

② The outline arrangement of special skills offers an apparent central theme to the resume that makes an introduction or summary less essential.

③ Recruitment skills are of great importance in a dynamic organization and her background as an executive recruiter is valuable in the several respects mentioned.

④ Standard employee job training skills are among her talents.

⑤ A more specialized training capability that relates to government regulations is also worth stressing.

⑥ Ability to function in a collective bargaining environment adds a whole new dimension to her qualifications.

⑦ A full range of regulatory compliance work from planning, to court cases, to complex reporting adds to her versatility and attractiveness as a candidate.

⑧ **Positions Held** supplies the specifics expected, but requires no elaboration.

⑨ Three working environments and orientations are apparent and valued.

⑩ An appropriate degree is listed matter-of-factly.

Rosemary P. Stuart

56 Meridian Avenue
Columbus, MS 39702
601-473-8976 (Office)
601-234-5565 (Residence)

Specialized Abilities

RECRUITMENT

- Experienced in defining hiring official needs both as an in-house personnel officer and as an executive recruiter.
- Capable of dealing effectively with executive search firms due to prior experience in that sector.

TRAINING

- Conducted new employee orientation and task training in financial, consulting, and retail settings.
- Trained managers on compliance with their obligations under EEO and other regulations affecting their departments.

LABOR RELATIONS

- Company representative during NLRB conducted vote on union representation for major retail chain.
- Benefits negotiator for bank holding company.

AFFIRMATIVE ACTION

- Designed and implemented EEO/AA programs at two large firms.
- Party to suits at the district court level.
- Coordinated state and federal reporting.

Positions Held

June 1987 - Present: Personnel Officer, Center Bank and Trust Company, New Orleans, LA.

January 1983 - May 1987: Recruiter, Dunhill Executive Search, Inc., Marysville, MS.

July 1980 - December 1983: Training Specialist, Bloomington Department Stores, Ltd., Canton, LA.

Education

Bachelor of Science
Business Administration
Pearl University, Arkansas, 1980

51. Pharmacist

FOCUSED RESUME

General Strategy

Ms. Brookings has a long history of steady, career-relevant employment, but wants to focus attention on her aggregate capabilities and achievements. This is best done by using the **Focused Resume** format.

This resume is designed to:

- pinpoint a discrete set of capabilities that she holds within her profession; and

- show a selected set of achievements that highlight her effectiveness.

Specific Points

1. **Overview** spells out the broad outline of her experience and states a general goal.

2. **Capabilities** provides a format in which highlighted skills are briefly outlined.

3. Within the profession, this is sufficient to relate the basic competencies.

4. Major retail management experience is unique and warrants mentioning.

5. Computer literacy as applied to the industry and buyer experience are also specialized skills not expected in the average pharmacist.

6. Consulting shows broader role and some authority professionally.

7. Achievements verify in tangible terms how effective she has been.

8. The range of acomplishments would be attractive to a major chain seeking a professional manager.

9. Employment shows the positions in which her achievements were made.

10. The appropriate degree underwrites her professional legitimacy.

Joyce C. Brookings

3098 Birch Lane
Bemidji, MN 56601
218-664-8957 (Office)
218-392-6032 (Residence)

(1) **Overview**: Fourteen year pharmacist with institutional and retail experience seeks management position in the pharmaceutical industry.

(2) **Capabilities**

- Licensed, degreed, board certified pharmacist. (4)

- Retail manger with successful supervision of multi-store operation.

(3) • Literate in the application of computers to the pharmaceutical trade.

- Extensive buying experience in both medications and sundries. (5)

- Consultant to hospitals and medical staffs on drug selection. (6)

Achievements

- National Retail Pharmacist of Year runner-up 1987.

(7) • Increased total prescription sales by 200 percent in three years. (8)

- Devised and implemented Cross-Check computerized prescription comparison system credited with identifying dozens of potentially serious medication conflicts monthly.

Employment

March 1985 - Present: Managing Pharmacist, MedPharm Drug Centers, Bemidji, MN.

(9) June 1980 - February 1985: Retail Pharmacist, Start Drugs, Washington, DC.

July 1976 - May 1980: Pharmacy Officer, Army Medical Corps, Devens Army Hospital, MA.

Education

Bachelor of Pharmacy
Brainerd University, MN
1976

(10)

52. Photographer

FOCUSED RESUME

General Strategy

Ms. Humphries is an independent free-lance photographer who wants to solicit further assignments on the basis of what she has done, but there is no formal job history to base it upon. Her best alternative is to construct a **Focused Resume** that will provide a reviewer with an easily read summary of:

- her technical capabilities;

- contacts in the business;

- lifestyle factors supportive of her career; and

- what she has done professionally.

Specific Points

(1) **Overview** is used to put herself into a worldly professional context and state her availability for further assignments.

(2) **Abilities** provides a summary of why she is capable of doing the job.

(3) Big league equipment and professional processing define her status.

(4) Press credentials, language capabilities, and comfort living overseas are all important in getting the pictures of world events.

(5) **Assignments** defines her work as a photographer and is divided into staff and free-lance—shows continued success in the independent mode.

(6) Diverse, challenging environments cited—Europe, Central America.

(7) Added dimension of covering events in Asia.

(8) Served her time successfully in the political trenches.

(9) Courage to work the inner city crime scene noted.

(10) Basic journalistic credential verified.

Debora K. Humphries
3 Fulton Street
Grand Rapids, MI 49503
616-243-2331 (Residence)

 Overview: Journalistic photographer with four years of international free-lance experience and sales to major news services seeking further affiliations in the capacity of an independent contractor.

Abilities

- Owner and expert user of Haselblad and Nikon cameras with a full complement of supporting equipment.

- Established relationships with principal commercial photo processing centers in New York.

- Fluent in European and Asian languages; raised overseas as a diplomatic dependent.

- Press credentials certified in major markets.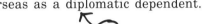

Assignments

<u>July 1988 - Present</u>: <u>Free-lance photo journalist</u>

- Fall 1989 — Eastern European coverage of liberation movements.

- Summer 1989 — Colombian drug war and other Central American issues.

- Spring 1989 — Peoples Republic of China student uprising.

- Fall 1988 — Photo feature contract on Japanese economy.

<u>June 1985 - July 1988</u>: <u>Staff Photographer, The Washington Post</u>

- Coverage of the Congress from the human perspective.

- Election coverage as a traveling journalist alternating parties.

- Crime in the nation's capital.

Education

Bachelor of Science
Journalism
Davidson College, MN 1985

53. Physician Assistant

WORK HISTORY RESUME

General Strategy

Ms. Reginald has a logical pattern of employment that is uncomplicated and career-supporting. Her choice of the **Work History Resume** is an appropriate one since it will allow her to:

- present her several credentials in the context of relevant work; and
- thoroughly describe the duties performed by health provider setting.

Specific Points

1. **Overview** sets the tone for her work history, which is more PA than RN—an important distinction to establish for her objective.

2. States her goal of entering a practice where her compensation will be more than a salary.

3. Education is dual-track—degree plus important certification.

4. Associate degree nurse status established—basis for achieving RN status.

5. MEDEX Certificate that qualifies her as a PA needs no further explanation within the community that will examine her credentials—it has the status of an additional degree.

6. **Employment** accounts for chronological continuity and describes duties in two settings.

7. PA and HMO points are made in this job description.

8. Actual tasks performed as a PA are outlined here.

9. Accounts for the time period and shows that PA training was full time.

10. Traditional nursing background is reaffirmed.

Cynthia L. Reginald, RN, PA

8 Rutherford Street
Boston, MA 02129
617-394-0038 (Office)
617-894-2934 (Residence)

①

Overview

Experienced health care professional with formal RN and
MEDEX/PA credentials, a year of nursing and 4 years as a PA.
Seeking to enter a private practice situation as a
② financially participating physician associate.

Education

Associate in Science   ③   MEDEX Certificate
Nursing   Physician Assistant
Greenfield Junior College, 1983   South Boston College, 1986

④   ⑤

Employment

June 1986 - Present: Physician Assistant, Boston Area Health
Management Association. One of 4 P.A.s assigned to Team 1 of ⑦
the HMO for the purpose of screening patients for primary
physician care. Conduct physical examinations and consult on
the results with the patients and, as appropriate,
physicians. Other duties include ordering lab tests, ⑧
diagnosing common maladies, and prescribing routine
⑥ treatments.

September 1984 - May 1986: Full-time MEDEX/PA training. ⑨

July 1983- August 1984: Hospital Nurse, Greater Boston
Presbyterian Hospital. General duty nurse responsible for
attending patients on the postoperative care ward.
Administered medication and therapeutic regimens prescribed
by physicians. Typical shift involved managing the care for
approximately 23 patients with the assistance of LPNs,
orderlies, and other floor staff. ⑩

54. Private Investigator

COMPETENCY CLUSTER RESUME

General Strategy

Ms. King is a law enforcement professional with several periods of traditional employment, but her most current one is in a self-employed capacity. She is more interested in showing what she can do than explaining why her business is not something she wants to continue. The most desirable way to combine her assets for an employer's evaluation is the **Competency Cluster Resume.**

The **resume** will be used primarily to:

- show that she can function as a law enforcement insider; and

- demonstrate that she can do the things that investigators are paid to do.

Specific Points

1. **Overview** instantly establishes her as qualified in both public and private sectors.

2. It also says what situation she seeks and where.

3. **Capabilities** highlight the three areas of primary competency.

4. Ties with the law enforcement establishment are established here.

5. Familiarity with the law on a practical level is confimed.

6. Evidence that she is capable of gathering information from the standard sources.

7. Important capabilities in the domestic investigations field are noted.

8. Ability to use photo and video equipment to document observations for possible use in court or in out-of-court settlements based on convincing evidence.

9. Employment history verifies claims to various kinds of experience.

10. An associate degree in criminology adds credibility.

Ida J. King
8 Wilson Lane
Laurel, MD 20707
301-723-8677 (Office)
301-889-2349 (Residence)

 Overview: Experienced law enforcement and security officer with police and licensed private investigator experience seeks affiliation with an established investigative firm in the Baltimore/Washington area.

Capabilities

<u>INSTITUTIONAL</u>

- Urban police officer in the capacities of patrolman and detective.
- Knowledge of enforcement and judicial bureaucracies.
- Acquainted with and respected by principals and functionaries throughout the regional law enforcement establishment.
- Working knowledge of civil and criminal statutes.

<u>RESEARCH</u>

- Government agency files.
- Telephone investigation.
- Personal interviewing.

<u>SURVEILLANCE</u>

- Domestic evidence gathering.
- Video and photographic techniques.
- Pursuit and documentation of movements.

Experience

<u>June 1987 - Present</u>:   Security Consultant, Self-employed.

<u>April 1981 - May 1987</u>: Detective, Baltimore Municipal Police Department, Baltimore, MD

<u>June 1978 - March 1981</u>: Patrolman, Columbia Police Department, Columbia, MD.

Education

Associate in Applied Science
Criminology
Hamilton Community College, MD, 1978

55. Product Manager

WORK HISTORY RESUME

General Strategy

Mr. Akrin is using the **Work History Resume** to portray his series of career-related professional positions. This approach is desirable in his case because the terminology, position titles, company names, etc. are all readily conceptualized by the potential reviewers of his resume.

This resume is designed to:

- state his overall qualifications and next career objective;

- detail each position held and describe the duties related to each; and

- demonstrate that he has the academic credentials on which to base his career.

Specific Points

(1) **Overview** briefly states his three areas of specialization and market segment.

(2) Next, it says that he is after more of the same on a higher level.

(3) **Experience** is a straightforward listing of career positions held and verifies that employment has been continuous.

(4) A significant position coupled with a successful initiative makes for a powerful introduction to his work history.

(5) Dollar volume is needed to portray the scope of his effort and responsibilities.

(6) Results are clearly demonstrated—verifiable by references.

(7) Position is enhanced by noting the industry position of his company.

(8) Numbers and kinds of people on his staff show the magnitude of the effort.

(9) Served his time on the road selling the products he now manages.

(10) An ideal combination of degrees to back his career.

William K. Akrin
56 Tura Road
Bennington, CT 48009
203-222-9988 (Office)
203-333-9075 (Residence)

Overover: Seven years of sales, market research, and product management experience in the consumer products retail segment. Seeking expanded opportunities as a product manager in a related industry.

Experience

November 1987 - Present: *Product Manager-Consumer Health Remedies, Milken & Trosper Pharmaceuticals, Inc., Bennington, CT.*

Led Milken back into the forefront of the analgesic market by generating contemporary health benefits strategies for existing products. Directed an $11 million campaign that included the design and implementation of test-marketing procedures, product packaging redesign, direct-mail sample delivery to selected target groups, and national advertising keyed to life-extension health philosophy. Resounding success confirmed by three-fold increase of market share that has been sustained for two years.

May 1984 - October 1987: *Market Research Analyst, Tifton-Williams Company, Trewsberry, CT*

Analyzed the market potential for dozens of retail consumables for the country's 3rd largest producer of personal care items. Directed a team of 2 statisticians, 2 clerical, and 4 area specialists in the evaluation and statistical testing of product receptivity in pre-defined markets. Credited with co-developing the targeted marketing scheme rapidly being viewed as the coming standard of the industry.

July 1982 - April 1984: *Sales Representative, National Home Products, Ltd., Stillwell, CT.*

One of 12 representatives selling consumer home cleaning and personal care products to retail outlets in the Southern New England region. In 18 months rose to the 2nd highest volume in the region and received the Outstanding New Salesman Award for 1984 for the Eastern Division.

Education

Bachelor of Science
Marketing
Smith University, 1980

Master of Business Administration
Marketing Concentration
Drexton University, 1982

56. Public Relations Specialist

FOCUSED RESUME

General Strategy

Mr. Bellman can do the job of a public relations person and he has the job success to prove it. What he wants to do is avoid repeating essentially the same job description three times in a standard resume. The answer to his dilemma is the **Focused Resume.** Using its format, he will be able to:

- graphically list the skills he has;

- back them with solid accomplishments that demonstrate their application; and

- underwrite it all with the right work history and college degree.

Specific Points

1. He opens the resume by targeting the precise position and level of authority he seeks.

2. Next the institution is classified as one that will provide a growth environment in which he can ply his trade.

3. **Skills** are those expected for the position and they are put forward without unnecessary elaboration—leave that for the interview.

4. **Accomplishments** are general as well, but do focus on things with which a college president—the person hiring him—will easily identify.

5. He can keep the alumni happy and contributing.

6. Was the best in the state at conceiving an effective promotion for his college.

7. Knows how to get the president visibility in popular academic media.

8. **Employment** shows continuity and progression.

9. The position he is coming from is a logical stepping stone to the kind for which he is making application.

10. An acceptable undergraduate degree is in evidence.

Rodney H. Bellman

98 Fairway Circle
Presque Isle, ME 04769
207-564-2323 (Office)
207-895-0267 (Residence)

Target Position

(1) Managing the public relations staff of a major university with full decision making responsibility. Institution should be rapidly growing or already established as a leader in its (2) sector.

Skills

(3)

- Speech preparation
- News release writing
- Media event coordination
- Publications creation
- Articulation of institutional image

Accomplishments

(4)

- Increased alumni participation by 23 (5) percent during two year directorship.
- Won the State Education Associations' (6) Promotion of the Year Award for 1985.
- Collection of President's speeches drafted by me published as a nationally (7) distributed monograph.

Employment

(9)

June 1987 - Present: Public Relations Officer, Montpelier University.

(8) February 1984 - May 1986: Director of Public Information, New England Association of Colleges and Schools. Freeburg, ME.

September 1982 - January 1984: Alumni Director, Lourdsburg College, Lourdsburg, ME.

Education

Bachelor of Science
Journalism
Smith University, 1982

(10)

57. Purchasing Agent

COMPETENCY CLUSTER RESUME

General Strategy

Ms. Johns has held two professional positions since graduating from college, but neither was for a very long period of time. She has good references, has learned important job-related skills, and wants to move on again. What is needed is the format of the **Competency Cluster Resume,** which can draw the reviewer's attention first to what she has to offer and, secondarily, to the brief tenure in her jobs.

The objective of this resume is to:

- present a capable person who knows what she wants and can demonstrate her ability to handle the task;

- graphically dominate the resume with desirable skills, highlighted and backed immediately with limited, supporting facts; and

- confirm work experience, proper college degree, and positions held.

Specific Points

① **Position Sought** says what she is after—including level of authority.

② Desired characteristics of the company are also noted.

③ **Competencies** form the heart of the resume—no need to hunt them from within several job descriptions.

④ Knows how to deal with suppliers in two primary situations.

⑤ Level of responsibility best shown by dollar value of transactions managed.

⑥ Important evidence that she can bargain and achieve savings.

⑦ Without great detail, this says she can buy for heavy industry—details can be provided upon request and would be the subject of discussion anyway.

⑧ Positions held tend to type her as what she claims to be.

⑨ Degree held is appropriate and also needs to be mentioned.

⑩ Key affiliation is an expectation in her field.

Mary Elizabeth Johns
42 Woodyard Drive
New Orleans, LA 70186
504-843-7886 (Office)
504-763-2133 (Residence)

(1) **Position Sought:** Group Purchasing Manager for commodities group in manufacturing environment with supervisory and purchase authorization responsibilities. Company should be currently profitable and growing. *(2)*

Competencies

Supplier Relations	• Attend national trade shows to develop contacts and current market knowledge. *(4)*
	• Receive visiting sales representatives and evaluate offerings.
Bid Acquisition	• Prepared $300,000 to $2 million commodity bidding events and managed the outcomes. *(5)*
Negotiation	• Achieved savings averaging 18 percent over industry tender prices for 3 commodity groups, 13 percent overall. *(6)*
Commodities	• Active in raw materials acquisition for heavy industrial components. *(7)*

(3)

Experience

(8) June 1987 - Present: General Purchasing Agent, Jones and Likeland Fabricators, Ltd. Gulf Coast City, LA.

July 1986 - May 1987: Commodities Buyer, Witson Manufacturing Company, Inc., New Carrolton, LA.

Education

(9) Bachelor of Science
Business Administration
Holy Saints University, 1986

Professional Affiliations

Member: National Association of Purchasing Managers

(10)

58. Real Estate Broker

FOCUSED RESUME

General Strategy

Ms. Garrett is in a very performance-oriented field—real estate sales. Less emphasis will be placed on a perfect chain of positions held and degrees earned than on what she has done and how well. The correct vehicle for highlighting her strengths as a sales person and sales manager is the **Focused Resume.**

This resume will accomplish the following:

- demonstrate in not too many words the fact that she is a sales producer; and

- show that she has the professional licenses, affiliations, and experience needed to do her job.

Specific Points

① **Overview** is used to headline what she is, has done, and is after.

② The position sought is qualified—has to be a national franchise affiliate.

③ **Capabilities** bullet her functional areas of expertise in the industry.

④ In a few phrases she ticks off the essentials for the position to which she aspires—elaboration will be left for the interview.

⑤ **Achievements** show how her basic skills have been applied successfully.

⑥ Lead item is personal productivity as a salesperson—over time, not just one good year.

⑦ Respectability, stature, and character reflected by state board appointment.

⑧ Quantified success in performance that relates directly to the task proposed.

⑨ **Experience** backs her claim to such levels of functioning in the business.

⑩ Mention of a degree cannot hurt, even if unrelated and nonessential.

Joan F. Garrett

21 Pine Lane
Bowling Green, KY 42101
502-834-9879 (Office)
502-547-8210 (Residence)

① **Overview:** Proven residential real estate sales producer and manager with eleven years of combined sales and brokerage experience seeks affiliation with major national franchise in a senior sales management capacity. ②

Capabilities ③

- Licensed Real Estate Broker
- Eleven years of successful, full-time, residential real estate sales ④
- Certified real estate appraiser
- Rental management experience
- Training of sales personnel

Achievements ⑤

- Annual sales in excess of $1.5 million for the past 5 years ⑥
- Elected professional representative to Kentucky Board of Realtors ⑦
- Managed nationally franchised office that led Central Region in sales volume growth in 1989. ⑧
- Sponsored and trained 94 of the Million Dollar Residential Round Table salesmen recognized in the Central Region in the last year.

Experience ⑨

<u>June 1985 - Present</u>: Residential Broker, Stallings Better Homes and Farms Realty, Inc., Bowling Green, KY.

<u>June 1978 - May 1985</u>: Real Estate Agent, Norwood Realty, Staunton, KY.

<u>July 1974 - May 1978</u>: English Teacher, Lexington Junior College, KY.

Education

Bachelor of Arts ⑩
English Literature
Western Kentucky University, 1974

59. Receptionist

COMPETENCY CLUSTER RESUME

General Strategy

Ms. Kyle is returning home with valuable experiences learned while spending a few years working in a large city. Neither her education nor job descriptions are anything noteworthy, so she wisely opts to feature her strengths in a **Competency Cluster Resume.**

The object of her resume is to:

- show that she can handle receptionist duties in a demanding setting; and

- affirm that she has already done so successfully and developed supporting skills in the course of gaining that experience.

Specific Points

① Since she has already left her last position, she lists only her home telephone number.

② **Overview** tells her situation and leads into her qualifications.

③ **Competencies** highlight the kinds of things for which the employer will be looking.

④ Telephone skills are absolutely essential—she establishes both technical competency and a measure of how trusted she has been (initial point of contact).

⑤ Without saying more than would be proper, she volunteers that she is indeed attractive and good with people—something the employer would want to know, but could otherwise not determine until the interview.

⑥ The ability to do more than answer phones is noted.

⑦ Some of these skills could promise upward mobility from the receptionist position.

⑧ **Experience** gives chronology and the employers suggest quality situations.

⑨ References could be noted, but she elects to hold them until interviewed.

⑩ Diploma is a desirable credential and subtle verification of regional linkage—they're not dealing with an uncomfortable outsider.

Carol H. Kyle

422 Haverhill Drive
Hutchinson, KS 67501
316-767-2843 (Residence) ①

Overview: Organizational receptionist returning to Kansas
② after five years of work experience in Washington seeks
opportunity to apply skills locally.

Competencies

③ TELEPHONE SKILLS ④

PERSONAL QUALITIES

CLERICAL SKILLS ⑥

Five years of PBX and key
system experience in
professional organizations of
more than 50 people.
Answered and referred calls
as the initial point of
contact.

Well groomed, attractive ⑤
woman with an excellent
professional manner and an
interest in people.

Type 60 WPM on conventional
or word processing equipment.
Filing, basic bookkeeping, ⑦
and other general office
skills.

Experience

June 1988 - December 1989: Receptionist, American
Association of Insurance Adjusters, Washington, DC.

⑧ April 1985 - May 1988: Receptionist, Criminal
Investigations Division, U. S. Department of Justice,
Washington, DC.

Education

⑨

Diploma
Office Management
Fort Hays Business School, 1985

⑩

60. Retail Buyer

FOCUSED RESUME

General Strategy

Ms. Napier is an accomplished buyer who is seeking another position because a merger is about to eliminate hers. She has spent her entire career with two firms and she would like to distance herself from that limited background. The best approach is for her to relegate the job history to the end of her resume and amplify her special abilities and accomplishments directly and early in a **Focused Resume.**

Her resume will achieve:

- an honest statement of her situation and desire to continue in her career elsewhere;

- a clear demonstration that she has the skills needed to do the job; and

- evidence that she can apply her talents successfully and profitably.

Specific Points

① Office phone listing is fine since her employer is assisting in her effort to relocate.

② **Overview** says what she seeks and what motivates her to change positions.

③ **Capabilities** make clear the fact that she has specific skills to offer.

④ Dollar values make it possible for a reviewer to place her on a scale of responsibility held.

⑤ Implications of national networking serve her purpose of breaking local image.

⑥ Foundation of retail experience is established.

⑦ **Achievements** show she is a rated performer nationally in her class store.

⑧ Regional recognition and successful major deal add to her stature.

⑨ **Experience** shows a chronology of work that backs her prior claims.

⑩ Marketing degree further confirms the appropriateness of her career preparation.

Janice W. Napier

398 South Akin Boulevard
Cedar Rapids, IA 52407
319-823-7690 (Office)
319-334-3254 (Residence)

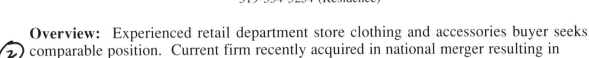

Overview: Experienced retail department store clothing and accessories buyer seeks comparable position. Current firm recently acquired in national merger resulting in staff consolidations.

Capabilities

• Clothing and accessories buying experience for a three store, family owned department store chain with annual sales of $20 million.

• Experienced participant in major trade shows presenting goods for the industry.

• Budget management for the $12 million clothing segment of the firm's annual sales.

• Proven observer of consumer buying trends.

• Extensive national contacts in the industry.

• Ten years of retail sales and sales management experience before becoming a buyer.

Achievements

• Top quartile performance in acquisitions/returns ratios for buyers in the $5-25 million departmental budget category nationally.

• Responsible for firm's successful adaptation to outlet pricing standards in the coat and outerwear garments segment.

• Twice selected Retail Buyer of the Year by the Iowa Retail Merchants' Association.

• Acquired price commitments on the Potter-Green jeans line before it achieved national status with resultant savings of $2.3 million.

Experience

June 1984 - Date: Clothing Buyer, Miller & Leget Department Stores, Cedar Rapids, IA.

June 1983 - May 1984: Clothing Sales Manager, Miller & Leget Department Stores, Cedar Rapids, IA.

July 1974 - May 1983: Women's Department Manager, Neeman's Fashions, Des Moines, IA

Education

Bachelor of Science (BS)
Business Administration (Marketing)
Des Moines University, 1974

61. Retail Salesperson

COMPETENCY CLUSTER RESUME

General Strategy

Ms. St. Clair is a top-level retail salesperson whose productivity would be overshadowed by an ordinary resume. It is important for her to distinguish herself from the image of a passive retail clerk and establish herself as an effective sales professional with her own particular strengths and methods. She is advised to do this in the format of the **Competency Cluster Resume** since it allows her to:

- graphically portray herself as someone special in retail selling;

- note the special situation to which she aspires; and

- drop the shop names necessary to affirm her elegant image.

Specific Points

① **Overview** says tersely what she is and precisely what she wants to become.

② **Particular Abilities** was chosen to complement the phrasing popular in the advertising images of the kinds of places she works—and to which her resume is appealing.

③ Marketing shows that she knows how to develop clients actively in the expensive goods segment.

④ Volume demonstrates that she can become a one-person profit center.

⑤ Presentation indicates basic retail skills cast in a special light.

⑥ Individualized marketing is again stressed.

⑦ Present position establishes the level of her sales practice.

⑧ Respectable tenure shows reliability in this less-than-stable class of worker.

⑨ Major national department store background provided excellent entry-level experience.

⑩ Formal training at a respected institution adds to professional image.

Ruth V. St. Clair

875 Washington Avenue
Muncie, IN 47305
317-585-9367 (Office)
317-585-7657 (Residence)

 Overview: Top retail saleswoman specializing exclusive women's wear seeks participating interest in established boutique in winter resort area.

 Particular Abilities

MARKETING
- Client base of 587 in exclusive women's store located in suburban mall.
- Developed by direct mail and personal contact.
- Files maintained on tastes, interests, sizes, etc.

VOLUME

- Average annual sales of $367,000 over the past five years.
- Client pattern established at tri-seasonal average of approximately $2,500 each.

PRESENTATION
- Experienced in window and store presentation of elegant merchandise.
- Specialty is individual presentation to top clients on an appointment basis.

Experience

June 1987 - Present: Senior Sales Associate, Elegant Shops, Ltd., Muncie, IN.

June 1983 - May 1987: Retail Sales Consultant, Exclusive Clothing Boutique, Chicago, IL.

December 1979 - May 1983: Retail Clerk, Women's Fashions, Bloomingdales Department Store, Washington, DC.

Education

Certificate
Merchandising
Indiana Fashion Institute, 1979

62. Robotic Engineer

WORK HISTORY RESUME

General Strategy

Mr. Wright has followed the expected career ladder within his profession and it is proper and effective for him to rely on the **Work History Resume** to display his abilities and accomplishments.

His resume is designed specifically to:

- show a chain of responsible employment in his technical specialty;
- indicate the caliber of companies with which he has been associated; and
- highlight his special skills and contributions.

Specific Points

(1) **Overview** authoritatively states his position in the industry and the fact that he is looking for an opportunity.

(2) **Experience** is formatted to emphasize the position held, employer, and duties.

(3) Level of responsibility is made clear with title and place in organization.

(4) Measures are given of how well his efforts have served the company.

(5) Scope of effort and responsibility are again shown with specific examples and numbers.

(6) Cites a key talent—ability to gain government contracts.

(7) Quantifies the magnitude of business generated so it can be easily appreciated.

(8) Makes the link to his junior officer days that laid the groundwork for present-day understanding of the industry and business procsses.

(9) Specific value of time spent on the approval side of bid process is illustrated.

(10) Powerful combination of technical degrees is self-explanatory.

Ned V. Wright

387 Streamside Lane
Twin Falls, ID 83303
208-977-6634 (Office)
208-788-3844 (Residence)

 Overview: Defense industry automation engineer with successful government and private sector experience in aviation-related robotics seeks growth opportunity in the applications area.

 Experience

June 1987 - Present: *Robotic Applications Engineer, Huge Aerospace*, Idaho City, ID

Chief engineering interface between the production and computer programming segments of the fixed wing avionics robotic production division. Responsible for coordinating and directing the resolution of technical challenges inherent in adapting production line electronics to automated control. Achieved successful implementation on 37 percent of the line within two years. Production increased 23 percent and defects dropped 74 percent during the final quarter of evaluation.

June 1983 - May 1987: *Mechanical Automation Engineer, Nanonectics, Ltd.*, Valley of the Angeles Industrial Complex, Los Angeles, CA.

Project leader for a 5 member team consisting of 2 engineers, 1 technician, and 2 clerical assistants tasked with preparing bids for federal government requests for proposals. Team generated and managed an average of 14 major proposals annually, assisted production department with staffing for contracts acquired, and served as project monitor in-house. Yielded an average of 5 successful bids annually resulting in aggregate contracts of $45 million dollars per year.

July 1979 - May 1983: *Engineering Officer, United States Air Force Systems Command*, Andrews Air Force Base, MD.

Staff technical expert leading a team of 6 engineering evaluators appraising the potential of automated weapons systems proposed for USAF consideration. Served as intermediate screening authority after conceptual interest had been established by senior managers. Feasibility of robotic applications to USAF mission requirements was the focus of the effort that yielded a 19 percent development approval rate over the three year life of the project.

Education

Associate in Science (AS)
Computer Science
Boise Junior College, ID, 1976

Bachelor of Science (BS)
Industrial Engineering
Idaho State College, ID, 1979

63. School Administrator

COMPETENCY CLUSTER RESUME

General Strategy

Mr. Varney has held a series of jobs as an educator that have prepared him for a senior administrative position. Rather than list the jobs and duties, he prefers to pull together what it all means in terms of being able to handle the job he is pursuing. His choice to do this is the **Competency Cluster Resume.**

The objective of his resume is to:

- telegraph the fact that he has the specific skills necessary—without the detail that might obscure their collective importance; and

- back his claim with enough brief specifics to illustrate that he can make his case.

Specific Points

1. **Executive Summary** is used to say: "I have what you need—here it is point by point."

2. He uses its headline format to convey both longevity and specific skills.

3. **Competencies** outlines the very things that concern the people who will evaluate him for the position—shows he knows what their priorities are.

4. Each point is made as a topic and then by specific, quantified example.

5. Both business and educational skills are addressed in a result-oriented format.

6. Awareness and involvement in the operational use of technology in learning is established.

7. Underlying teaching skills are reaffirmed—did his time in the classroom.

8. Respect for the importance of community relations is illustrated.

9. Collective bargaining experience may well be essential and a basis for eliminating unsuccessful candidates early in the screening process—make the point, however briefly.

10. Experience and degrees are essential, but matter-of-fact.

Dennis S. Varney
795 Carlyle Street
Kewanee, IL 61443
309-499-0988 (Office)
309-877-2132 (Residence)

① Executive Summary

② • Public school administrator with 10 years of administrative and 5 years of teaching experience.
• Significant budget, community relations, and unionized teacher management experience.

Competencies

ADMINISTRATION

• Principal of a 2000 student, 100 faculty public secondary school in a suburban environment.
• Vice Principal of a 1500 student, 70 faculty rural intermediate school.

BUDGET

• Responsible for the preparation and management of a $5 million school budget.
• Planned and implemented a $1.7 million school renovation.
• Fiscal oversight for community generated non-taxpayer $980 million fund for school improvements.

③ ⑤ ④

CURRICULUM

• Implemented computer assisted math and reading instruction in a 500 teacher urban system. ⑥

TEACHING

• High school mathematics teacher in urban and suburban settings for 5 years before entering administration. ⑦

COMMUNITY RELATIONS

• Led successful bond drives in 2 communities resulting in major construction and renovation funding. ⑧

LABOR RELATIONS

• Senior district representative for 2 suburban systems with successful no-strike negotiations concluded in both instances. ⑨

Experience

<u>September 1985 - Present</u>: Principal, Suburban High School, Canton, IL.

<u>June 1980 - August 1985</u>: Vice Principal, Macon County High School, New Bedford, IL.

<u>June 1979 - May 1980</u>:   Consulting Curriculum Leader, Intercity School System, Wilmington, IL.

⑩ <u>June 1978 - May 1979</u>: Mathematics Teacher, Millmount High School, East Millmount, IL.

<u>August 1975 - May 1978</u>: Mathematics Teacher, Southside Intermediate School, Westwood, IL.

Education

Bachelor of Science (BS)
Math Education
Central Illinois University, 1975

Master of Science (MS)
Public School Administration
Central Illinois University, 1988

64. School Guidance Counselor

FOCUSED RESUME

General Strategy

Mr. Sandsome wants to present his credentials as an established educator with a clear focus on his guidance counselor attributes. Rather than list jobs and follow with the usual paragraph of duties, he has selected the **Focused Resume** as the vehicle for communicating a more directed message.

The goal of this resume is to:

- focus the reviewer's attention on the specific qualities associated with the counselor's role in a school;

- substantiate claims to effectiveness with examples of specific achievements; and

- underline the presentation with solid experience and training credentials.

Specific Points

1. A specific position is being sought, so it is designated at the head of the resume.

2. **Abilities** is used to tick off the expected and insert some special talents related to the job in question.

3. Substance abuse in schools is a major concern and he has experience dealing with it.

4. Initiative shown in going beyond government sources of financial aid.

5. Practical outreach to the community is a valuable asset.

6. Results are available to back claims of effectiveness in all areas.

7. Ideas have been good enough to institutionalize—projects he started now have a life of their own and reach beyond his area of influence.

8. Evidence of stature given by involvement with a national organization.

9. The right working experiences for the role he seeks.

10. Degrees appropriate to his aspirations.

Wadsworth T. Sandsome

35 North Island Drive
Haleiwa, HI 96740
808-675-8345 (Office)
808-776-9078 (Residence)

Position Sought

Director of Counseling Services

Abilities

- State Certified School Guidance Counselor.
- Specialized training in the recognition and treatment of adolescent substance abuse.
- In-depth familiarity with the use of computer databases designed to aid students in the selection of appropriate colleges and majors.
- Experienced group counseling leader.
- Knowledge of private as well as public sources of college bound student financial aid.
- Extensive work with private sector community work-study arrangements.

Achievements

- 80 percent of counselees admitted to college of their choice for the past five years.
- Awarded Parents' Club Award for Excellence 1989 in appreciation for efforts to establish private sector linkage between North Shore School and the burgeoning hospitality industry.
- Founder of Island Helpers Teen Substance Abuse Hotline that serves 3500 callers weekly.
- Summer Consulting Fellow to College Boardroom, a non-profit organization that designs career planning software for students.

Experience

<u>June 1987 - Present</u>: Guidance Counselor, North Shore High School, Kawela Bay, HI.

<u>June 1983 - May 1987</u>: Counselor, Kanehoe Intermediate School, Kanehoe, HI.

<u>July 1979 - May 1983</u>: History Teacher, Pearl Harbor High, Pearl City, HI.

Education

Bachelor of Science (BS)
Social Studies Education
University of Maryland, 1977

Master of Education (MEd)
Guidance and Counseling
University of Hawaii, 1983

65. Secretary

COMPETENCY CLUSTER RESUME

General Strategy

Ms. Andersen's two periods of employment have given her more than a simple listing of duties and dates would indicate. When combined with her education, they provide the basis for describing a very attractive array of skills. In order to bring this to the immediate attention of potential employers, she has selected the **Competency Cluster Resume** to showcase her assets.

Her resume is specifically designed to:

- portray the professionalism with which she views herself;

- list the specific skills and traits that give her claim substance; and

- define the career path she hopes to pursue.

Specific Points

① **Overview and Objective** set her resume above the average for such applicants by classifying her interests as professional and executive—only appropriate because she can substantiate the claim.

② Clear implication that she is looking for an opportunity to do more than be a secretary—administrative management is her goal and that will appeal to an employer seeking to develop such a person.

③ Her degree is specific and valuable—it gets prominent placement.

④ **Professional Skills** is the wording chosen to highlight her talents and cast them in a more important light.

⑤ The outline of skill topics tells a potential employer that she has the kind of comprehensive talent that can be considered for serious responsibility.

⑥ It is made clear that she is in command of modern office technology.

⑦ Knowledge of hiring procedures and regulatory requirements are apt to be valued by the executive she would support.

⑧ Ability to make business arrangements is a vital skill worth featuring.

⑨ **Experience** shows continuity of employment.

⑩ Current position verifies executive secretary stature.

Lynn J. Andersen

973 Albacort Circle
Savannah, GA 31407
912-929-6479 (Office)
912-938-7783 (Residence)

Overview and Objective

(1)

Professional Secretary with six years of advanced office services experience
seeks Executive Secretary position with potential for assuming
an administrative management role.

(2)

Education

(3)

Associate in Science (AS)
Secretarial Science
Metropolitan Community College, GA, 1983

Professional Skills (4)

OFFICE MANAGEMENT
- Coordination of office clerical routine.
- Schedule management.
- Vendor liaison with suppliers of services.

DOCUMENT PREPARATION
- 60 WPM using electric typewriter or word processing equipment.
- Advanced user of principal word processing software packages.

EQUIPMENT OPERATION
- Personal computers and associated peripheral equipment.
- Fax and modems.

(5)

(6)

DICTATION/TRANSCRIPTION
- 60 WPM vocal dictation.
- Accomplished transcriber.

PERSONNEL
- Preparation and placement of advertising.
- Applicant response, appointment arrangements, EEO record keeping.

(7)

EXECUTIVE ASSISTING
- Planning of meetings and conferences, locally and at remote sites.
- Arranging business travel.
- Screening and appointment management.

(8)

Experience

(9)

November 1987 - Present: Secretary to the Director of Marketing, Rockaway ← (10)
Manufacturing Company, Ltd., Savannah, GA.

May 1983 - October 1987: Secretary, Jensen & Jensen Management Consultants, Tyron,
GA.

66. Securities Broker

COMPETENCY CLUSTER RESUME

General Strategy

Ms. Proper has an employment history that shows only one relevant position, although her skills are really very well developed. She has decided that a **Competency Cluster Resume** will do a far more graphic job of displaying her strengths than would a bland position listing and description.

Her resume is intended to:

- show that she is an established and successful salesperson in the financial products field;

- prove that she has the professional attributes to practice her trade; and

- show that she has obtained the education to support her career change.

Specific Points

① **Executive Summary** establishes what she has done and in what market segment.

② It further states her goal to become a partner in a securities firm.

③ Professional certification is immediately verified—no one needs to train her.

④ She brings with her a specialty in the broad field of investment products.

⑤ A base of buying clients is already established and likely to follow.

⑥ She can demonstrate serious levels of productivity.

⑦ Proof is offered that she can generate new business as well.

⑧ Brokerage experience is anchored in a respected firm.

⑨ Prior teaching experience is noted matter-of-factly.

⑩ Education shows commitment to the business career.

Sandra K. Proper

1987 Clearpond Way
Miami Shores, FL 33138
305- 966-0980 (Office)
305-877-2167 (Residence)

Executive Summary

① Proven exceptional productivity in the retail marketing of investment products to young professionals with performance sustained over a six year period. Objective is to attain participating partner status in a compatible firm. ②

Professional Abilities

LICENSURE

③ • Securities and Exchange Commission licensed retail broker

PRODUCT SPECIALIZATION

• No Load Mutual Funds ④
• Emerging Growth Stocks
• College Tuition Fund Plans

CLIENTS ⑤

• Young professionals

PRODUCTION

⑥ • Achieved $2 million in annual sales in third year; sustained through sixth year.
⑦ • Business development activities yielded 54 purchasing clients last quarter.

Experience

⑧ <u>June 1983 - Present</u>: Retail Stock Broker, Blackmund Investing Associates, Ltd., Miami, FL.

⑨ <u>August 1981 - May 1983</u>: Teacher, Kevinville Schools, Kevinville, CA.

Education

Bachelor of Arts (BA)
Art History
Smith University, AL 1981

Master of Science (MS) ⑩
Business Administration
University of West Florida, 1988

67. Security Manager

FOCUSED RESUME

General Strategy

Mr. Cooper has had a long and complete work history, but he feels his attributes will be better shown if pulled from the individual job descriptions where they are to be found. He selected the **Focused Resume** because it lets him place the attention wanted on certain skills and traits that are the selling points of his profession.

This resume is designed to:

- paint an overall picture of an experienced professional whose talents stem from a number of work experiences;

- show achievements that demonstrate excellence in his field; and

- back it with responsible experience and relevant educational achievement.

Specific Points

1. **Overview** sketches the experienced security practitioner and the goal he seeks.
2. **Capabilities** lists specific assets that should be valued by private security firms.
3. Basic qualifying items are affirmed.
4. Special skills are identified.
5. Public relations and management experience is noted.
6. **Achievements** are the kind apt to be appreciated in his trade.
7. Character reference items are also included.
8. Ability to generate business is important to note.
9. Experience validates claims made earlier in resume.
10. Education is a nice concluding touch of professionalism—not a mandatory degree.

John V. Cooper

3976 98th Street, SW
Washington, DC 20098
202-992-7845 (Office)
202-765-2116 (Residence)

(1) Overview

Successful security officer and manager with experience in military, municipal, and private security settings seeks senior management position with private firm.

(2) Capabilities

- Licensed private investigator
- Military security police training and experience
- (3) Advanced martial arts training
- 5 years experience as a municipal police officer (4)
- 6 years as a private investigator
- Expert firearms instructor
- (5) Experienced speaker before community groups
- Proven security organization manager

Achievements

- Regional NRA pistol champion
- Appointed to state licensing board for private investigators (7)
- (6) Deacon of the Midlands Methodist Church
- 4 time regional Karate champion
- Security consultant to industry and government
- Increased account dollar volume 45 percent in current position (8)

Experience

(9) <u>June 1987 - Present</u>: Director of Domestic Investigations, Blue Diamond Detective Agency, Inc., Washington, DC.

<u>June 1983 - May 1987</u>: Self-Employed Private Investigator, Bethesda, MD.

<u>July 1978 - May 1983</u>: Patrolman, Alexandria Police Department, Alexandria, VA.

<u>May 1975 - June 1978</u>: Army Military Police, California and Germany.

Education

Associate in Applied Science (AAS)
Law Enforcement Technology
Washington Area Technical College, DC, 1984

(10)

68. Teacher Aide

COMPETENCY CLUSTER RESUME

General Strategy

Ms. Sherington is a teacher aide without a particularly impressive list of jobs held. What she does have is a composite set of experiences that will be viewed with respect by someone looking for a competent assistant in the classroom. To present her skills more attractively, she has decided to use the **Competency Cluster Resume.**

The tasks to be accomplished by this resume are to:

- show a combination of life experiences and training that qualify her to serve as a paraprofessional teacher; and

- back the claims with character, educational, and working experiences that will give her claims substance.

Specific Points

(1) Present position is part-time and rather informal so she elects to be called at home, rather than at an office where the response might be uncertain.

(2) **Summary and Objective** states what she wants to do and qualifications.

(3) Skills are grouped in such a manner as to address the main concerns of the potential hiring official.

(4) Where possible, institutional experience is shown first and then further supported by less formal, in-the-home experience.

(5) Specific classroom assisting tasks are listed and can be verified.

(6) Classroom management assistance is probably what is needed most in the setting to which she aspires.

(7) Supporting skills: first aid and awareness of childhood health concerns.

(8) Personal character is important and must be established.

(9) **Experience** frames the chronology of her adult life and lists relevant, if less than full-time experience.

(10) The college certificate will strengthen her claim to competency and appeal to those who work in a highly credential-oriented field like teaching.

Helen M. Sherington

104 Sandstone Road
Wilmington, DE 19802
302-977-9887 (Residence)

Summary and Objective

Experienced, formally trained paraprofessional with
young children in pre-school educational settings seeks
full-time public school position as a teacher's aide at the
kindergarten or grades 1-3 level.

Relevant Skills

CHILD-CARE

- Assisted in the operation of a 23
  child church day-care center for 2
  years
- Privately cared for 4 pre-school
  children at my residence for 3
  years

CLASSROOM MANAGEMENT

- Prepared art project materials
- Assisted with math and reading
  drills
- Arranged rest areas
- Led game activities
- Typed and reproduced materials

HEALTH CARE

- Certified in Red Cross First Aid
- Trained in early childhood health

PERSONAL CHARACTER

- Married mother of two teenagers
- 10 year resident of this community
- Active in community affairs
- Extensive references available

Experience

June 1987 - Present: Day-care Center Assistant, United
Lutheran Church, Beltsville, DE.

June 1985 - May 1987: Private day-care provider at my
residence.

July 1975 - May 1985: Housewife and mother.

Education

Certificate
Child-Care
Beacon Junior College, DE 1986

69. Technical Writer

WORK HISTORY RESUME

General Strategy

Mr. Akrin has several positions that constitute the sum total of his working experience and they are the context of his achievements. He decided that the best approach for him was to present a simple, but thorough, **Work History Resume** that would do a good job of:

- showing that he is a competent technical writer with the background to function at a computer user–oriented magazine; and

- detailing the kinds of training and experience that show technical preparation for this kind of writing.

Specific Points

① **Overview** frames the experience, training, and aspirations of the applicant.

② **Experience** is arrayed in such a manner as to break out the two positions, separate them by full-time study, and provide continuity to the brief section.

③ The Brainware position establishes him as a technical writer in the industry.

④ It also notes experience that would parallel the kinds of areas covered by a user-magazine writer—national workshops, instructions for laymen, etc.

⑤ The study break should be shown—keeps the chronology unbroken.

⑥ The Matson position shows that he has the technical expertise for his writing.

⑦ Worked directly with users—indicative of sensitivity to their interests.

⑧ User magazines really serve as a link between users and manufacturers, so these experiences are probably going to be attractive to the person hiring.

⑨ The technical expertise is well addressed educationally by his associate degree.

⑩ The bachelor's degree in technical writing completes the ideal credentials.

William K. Akrin

56 Tura Road
Bennington, CT 48009
203-222-9988 (Office)
203-333-9075 (Residence)

Overview

Technical Writer with formal training and experience in computer technology and technical writing seeks editorial opportunity with mass market user's magazine.

Experience

January 1985 - Present: Technical Writer
Brainware Computer Products, Inc., Bennington, CT.

Assist in the preparation of technical manuals that support the use of software products created at Brainware. Experience includes interviewing programmers and systems engineers to identify program features. Convey features and step-by-step instructions for use in lay language. Attend national workshops to receive feedback on manuals and products. Full range of mass market software including desktop publishing, graphic arts, and business packages featuring word processing, data bases, spread sheets, etc.

September 1982 - December 1985

Full-time study for Bachelor's degree.

June 1980 - August 1982: Customer Service Technician
Matson Software, Ltd., Norwich, CT.

Telephone contact for users of Matson Software products including their complete line of word processing, spread sheet, graphic presentation, and data base programs. Assisted users in isolating their problems and guiding them to solutions. Maintained records on nature of questions addressed and assisted technical writing staff in the revision of manuals.

Education

Associate in Arts (AA)
Computer Studies
Asnutuck Junior College, CT, 1980

Bachelor of Technology (BT)
Technical Writing
West Connecticut College, CT, 1987

70. Telecommunications Specialist

COMPETENCY CLUSTER RESUME

General Strategy

Mr. Goodwell feels that his worth exceeds the sum total of the two job descriptions that he would be presenting with a standard resume. With his technical orientation and the specific nature of his services, he chose to portray himself in the aggregate using a **Competency Cluster Resume.**

The objective of his resume is to:

- place in bold relief the several highly marketable things that he can do; and

- back it up with job settings and strong educational credentials that imply that he has the substance to deliver.

Specific Points

(1) **Overview** is used to sketch experience, indicate goal, and show confidence in his ability to thrive in a performance-based pay environment.

(2) **Areas of Competency** as a topic group draws the reviewer immediately to the productive substance of what he can do, not a mere job description.

(3) Examples briefly show levels of technology and markets where they are used.

(4) Not tied to a single vendor—broader, more independent status established.

(5) Demonstrates hands-on field service experience useful in his proposed role.

(6) Ability to implement and manage user services is evidenced here.

(7) Consulting experience is verified.

(8) Sales experience is noted as well as implied knowledge of the major provider's products and operation.

(9) An applied associate degree is presented.

(10) A specialized technical bachelor's degree caps his formal credentials.

Bernard K. Goodwell

76 La Junta Drive
Colorado Springs, CO 80908
719-332-0983 (Office)
719-776-8955 (Residence)

① **Overview**: Six years of designing and marketing commercial telecommunications services. Seeking growth opportunity in the western United States. Receptive to performance-based compensation arrangement in consulting or end-user applications.

Areas of Competency

NEEDS EVALUATION

- Assessment of voice, fax, data, and video requirements in banking, insurance, manufacturing and government environments. ③
- Appraisal of volume, costs, and best use of technology.

② EQUIPMENT SELECTION

- Independent perspective based on solid technical education and international industry familiarity.
- Established contacts with major vendors. ④

SERVICES SELECTION

- Knowledgeable in the available contractible services sectors, both majors and independents.

INSTALLATION

⑤ • Supervised the installation of 25 to 500 set, multifunction telecommunications systems.

OPERATION

⑥ • Managed the user training programs of all installations sold.

Experience

⑦ <u>June 1987 - Present</u>: Telecommunications Consultant, Buena Vista Technical Consulting, Ltd., Boulder, CO.

⑧ <u>July 1983 - May 1987</u>: Commercial Services Sales Representative, Mountain States Telephone, Denver, CO.

Education

Associate in Science (AS)
Digital Electronics
Mead Community College, AZ 1980
⑨

Bachelor of Science (BS)
Telecommunications
State University of Colorado 1983
⑩

71. Television Support Technician

FOCUSED RESUME

General Strategy

Ms. Arnold is seeking recognition in a combination technical and artistic specialty where specific abilities and experience are more important than job listings and duties performed. In order to make the most of her attributes, she has elected to present her record in the **Focused Resume** format.

The tasks to be accomplished by the resume are to:

- show an aggregate of skills gained in several settings that, together, have a greater value than their individual parts; and

- provide the concrete employment and training structure to show that she has been consistently productive within the industry.

Specific Points

(1) **Overview** begins with award-winning status and moves on to touch segments of the industry worked.

(2) Her objective is also presented in the opening statement.

(3) **Professional Abilities** outlines the categories of technical and artistic skill that the reviewer would be laboring to pick from a less pointed resume.

(4) The kinds of productions supported must be made clear.

(5) Status on the production team speaks to authority and role.

(6) Industry-recognized awards cast their glow on those who worked on their more mundane production aspects as well as the stars and producers—claim credit when due.

(7) **Achievements** is the section that tangibly confirms excellence.

(8) Union cards are so important that they legitimately constitute an achievement.

(9) A team player on award-winning productions.

(10) Employment record and the education credential round out her picture of overall competence.

Margaret A. Arnold

89 University Drive
Santa Marina, CA 93455
805-886-1903 (Office)
805-876-3921 (Residence)

(1) ## Overview

Award-winning Television Support Technician with national experience in multiple aspects of professional news, talk show, and drama productions seeks network or national cable opportunity. (2)

Professional Abilities

- SET MANAGEMENT — 6 years of experience in the management of set activities supporting news, talk show, and dramatic television productions. ←(4)

- LIGHTING — 4 years as associate lighting director for a producer of nationally syndicated television musical productions. Accomplished user of Kludge and special effects lighting in television applications. ←(5)

(3)

- SET DESIGN — 3 years professional and 5 years amateur set design. Professional years included assistant background construction director for the Emmy Award winning docudrama *War and Space*. (6)

(7) ## Achievements

(8) • Union cards held in the areas of television stage management, lighting, and set design.

(9) • On the staff of 7 production companies that received national industry recognition for excellence during my tenure.

- 1988 Audience Appreciation Award winner for set design in the live audience participation Minnie Walker Talk Show series.

Experience

<u>June 1983 - Present</u>: Set Manager, Gordon Boxwood Studios, Hollywood, CA.

<u>June 1982- May 1983</u>: Set Design Specialist, KNBB, Santa Clarita, CA.

<u>July 1979 - May 1982</u>: Lighting Technician, Samuel Whitworth Production Company, Los Angeles, CA.

(10)

Education

Associate in Science (AS)
Electronics Technology
Allan Whetstone Junior College, CA 1979

72. Training-and-Development Specialist

WORK HISTORY RESUME

General Strategy

Dr. Burnside has a unique situation that can be strongly presented in a traditional format—his special talent has been the direct outgrowth of a specific series of occupational experiences that describe him well. He has chosen the **Work History Resume** to paint a well-ordered picture of his somewhat unusual situation.

The objective of his resume is to establish that:

- he has a successful consulting practice that would be an attractive affiliation for an established training organization; and

- it all stems from a totally verifiable and respectable rise through traditional professional positions.

Specific Points

(1) Affirms his status, specialty, and what he is seeking in a brief **Overview.**

(2) **Experience** section is used to show how he put his consulting practice together while pursuing a traditional career.

(3) It begins with a description of his current practice.

(4) Evidence is presented of the growing demand and established reputation.

(5) Shows how he remained in the mainstream while completing his doctorate and establishing a consulting business.

(6) A solid base of traditional experience and the source of inspiration for his consulting orientation.

(7) His publications would be important to those considering adding him to their stable of authoritative presenters.

(8) His basic degrees are now important background for his consulting field.

(9) The doctor's degree lends authority to his presentations and writing.

(10) Comments explain that he is offering a share of his proven product if an established organization will free him to pursue his specialty.

Robert J. Burnside, Ph.D.
233 Eastwood Street
Beebe, AR 72012
501-883-7913 (Office)
501-989-2244 (Residence)

 Overview: Established national sales and motivation trainer seeks affiliation with a major consulting firm based in the Southeastern United States.

 Experience

<u>June 1987 - Present</u>: **Independent Training Consultant, Robert J. Burnside, Ph.D., Inc.**, Beebe, AR. Published "The Burnside System for Sales and Motivation" and toured nationally promoting its use in the selling industry. A 2-day seminar was structured and presented at 62 companies and 6 national sales meetings during the past two years. Future schedule includes 37 commitments with deposits. Strong interest expressed in follow-on presentations at advanced level.

<u>June 1979 - November 1987</u>: **Adjunct Faculty Member, Beebe Area Community College**. Taught adult evening courses in career decision making and small business start-up skills while completing dissertation, writing, and establishing independent consulting firm in industrial training.

<u>July 1970 - May 1979</u>: **Industrial Arts Teacher, Thurmont High School**, Casey, AR. Taught shop courses to high school students seeking positions in industry. Earned masters degree part time during this period, then began evening employment as a trainer in local industries. Developed insights regarding motivation and success and began doctoral studies in counseling.

National Publications

The Burnside System, 1987
Selling in the Professional Market, 1988

Education

Bachelor of Arts (B.A.)		Master of Education (M.Ed.)
Teacher Education		Industrial Arts
Smith University, TX, 1970		Arkansas State University, 1973

Doctor of Philosophy (Ph.D.)
Counseling
Florida University, 1980

Comments

The reason for seeking affiliation is that the growth in demand for my services precludes the timely development of follow-on products that have great potential. Willing to exchange partial rights for business management of my seminar business.

73. Travel Agent

FOCUSED RESUME

General Strategy

Ms. Winters is a very productive travel agent with a special set of skills that she wants to present very clearly. The prospect of listing jobs and duties is not appealing and would not do her justice. She is advised to use a **Focused Resume** to make the most of her brief but appealing presentation.

The objective of her resume is to:

- describe a geographic travel specialty that she has developed into an attractive and profitable niche; and

- verify that her claim is substantive—complete with productivity figures.

Specific Points

1. Her **Objective** states what she is trying to achieve in terms interesting to the potential recipients of her resume.

2. It also identifies the specialty that she is promoting—Alaskan group travel.

3. **Capabilities** tells just exactly what she can deliver—and does so briefly.

4. Ability to take her presentations to her potential customers is noted.

5. Experienced tour leader adds to the appeal.

6. Willing and able to handle the essential routine.

7. Experienced in coordinating with other travel professionals.

8. **Accomplishments** proves she can deliver—meaningful specifics given.

9. Yeoman experience in the industry is a matter of verifiable record.

10. Possesses some formal training in the business.

Suzanne V. Winters

4111 Providence Avenue
Fairbanks, AK 99702
907-747-9002 (Office)
907-776-7566 (Residence)

①

Objective — Affiliation with a major mainland chain or franchise
as a specialist in the promotion of Alaskan group travel. **②**

Capabilities

④

③

• Lower-48-states sales presentations to promote Alaska agency sponsored
activities

• Group presentations to civic and business groups

• Group tour leadership ← **⑤**

• Associated travel office routine and clerical responsibilities ← **⑥**

• Liaison with affiliated agencies internationally ← **⑦**

Accomplishments

• Personally responsible for the sale of $278,000 in group travel from mainland
and Hawaii affiliates in 1988.

⑧ • Initiated program of cooperative promotion with State Tourism Agency that has
yielded 1823 referrals in the first 8 months of operation.

• Designed custom tour for environmental groups following oil spill that attracted an
aggregate of 483 travelers in a 6 month period.

Experience

⑨ <u>June 1987 - Present</u>: *Travel Consultant*, Ask Mr. Williams Agency, Fairbanks, AK.

<u>June 1983 - May 1987</u>: *Travel Agent*, Express Independent Travel, Ltd., Anchorage,
AK.

Education

Certificate in Travel and Tourism
Anchorage Business College, AK 1983

⑩

74. Veterinary Technician

COMPETENCY CLUSTER RESUME

General Strategy

Mr. Kline is a specialized animal health paraprofessional whose talents lend themselves well to presentation under the format of the **Competency Cluster Resume.** While his attributes would be there to find in a more traditional resume, this approach brings them together for greater impact.

His resume is crafted specifically to:

- show a large-animal veterinarian that he has the groups of skills that can form clear profit centers in his practice; and

- substantiate the claim with specific examples, impressive experience, and legitimate professional credentials.

Specific Points

1. **Overview and Objective** classify the candidate and say what he wants to do and where.

2. AVMA certification of his program makes him instantly credible.

3. Routine vet paraprofessional skills are recounted.

4. Specialized skills like AI are added attractions.

5. Emergency field treatment qualifications will appeal to his market—the large-animal vet.

6. Working experience as a staff vet on a major ranch is of substantial value.

7. Previous experience in private practice is desirable.

8. Student experience was with the industry.

9. The associate degree qualifies him for his specialty.

10. The special quality of his degree is its AVMA certification—a point worth highlighting both here and under **Professional Abilities.**

Cary J. Kline, Jr.
788 Overpass Drive
Glendale, AZ 85301
602-345-9878 (Office)
602-667-6483 (Residence)

Overview and Objective

Large animal veterinary technician with over 6 years experience in the treatment of commercial beef cattle seeks private practice affiliation in the Southwestern United States.

Professional Abilities

- Graduate of American Veterinary Medical Association (AVMA) program

- Trained in large animal care

- Experienced in the administration of medication and vaccinations

- Artificial insemination specialist ← ④

- Surgical assisting

- Emergency field treatment of farm animals ← ⑤

- X-Ray and laboratory procedures

Experience

<u>June 1987 - Present</u>: *Veterinary Technician*, Queen Ranch, Glendale, AZ.

<u>June 1983 - May 1987</u>: *Veterinary Technician*, Davidson Large Animal ← ⑦ Clinic, Glendale, AZ.

<u>July 1981 - May 1983</u>: *Seasonal employment* in the commercial cattle ⑧ finishing industry of Northern Arizona as a work-study student in veterinary technology.

Education

⑨

Associate in Applied Science (AAS)
Veterinary Technology
An AVMA Approved Program of Study
⑩ Community College of Tucson, 1983

75. Word-Processing Operator

COMPETENCY CLUSTER RESUME

General Strategy

Ms. McDaniel has a narrow specialty and a specific goal in mind. Her strongest presentation format is the **Competency Cluster Resume** because it will allow her to:

- separate herself from the secretarial stereotype by graphically featuring her very specialized talents; and

- package it in such a manner as to convey both special skills and traditional preparation including clerical experience and formal training.

Specific Points

(1) **Overview** tells the reviewer that a very specific situation is being sought.

(2) The specialization involves both the word-processing product and the fact that the applicant aspires to a training role.

(3) Identifies the product and systems in order to allow effective employer screening and save the inconvenience of an interview by an inappropriate employer.

(4) Mentions the mail-merge and other tasks that can be efficiently done.

(5) Associate the capability with the most modern office technology—that based on telecommunications by fax and modem.

(6) Mentions the ability to support tabular and graphics applications.

(7) Speed in entering data remains an important attribute.

(8) Supporting software that enhances the final product is valuable to cite.

(9) Experience in the clerical environment is established.

(10) Formal training underwrites her practical skills.

Anna P. McDaniel

2909 Phoenix Avenue
Montgomery, AL 36196
205-727-5990 (Office)
205-884-1243 (Residence)

Overview

① Single product word-processing specialist with in-depth capabilities in the production and handling of business correspondence and documents in all formats. Seeking large office environment where production activities can be ② supplemented by the training and supervision of others.

Word-Processing Capabilities

③ • Expert user of Microsoft Word on Macintosh and IBM systems.

④ • Mail-merge specialist experienced in the custom mailing of personalized correspondence.

⑤ • Highly competent in the sending, receipt, and reformatting of electronically transmitted documents.

• Accomplished in the integration of tabular data and graphics into word-processing documents. ⑥

⑦ • 80 WPM for text entry.

⑧ • Thorough familiarity with the use of spell-check and other supporting software.

• Extensive laser printer experience as well as tractor fed forms and label printers.

Experience

June 1987 - Present: Word-Processing Specialist
Alabama Northern Electrical Cooperative, Enterprise, AL.

⑨ June 1983 - May 1987: Secretary
Alabama Association of Real Estate Appraisers, Montgomery, AL.

Education

⑩ Diploma in Secretarial Science
Enterprise Community College, AL 1983

4 COVER LETTERS AND INTERVIEWS

Preparation of the resume is only part of the process of getting hired. A poor resume can hurt you. A good one can help. But the end result depends on your ability to integrate the resume into an overall job search process that is well conceived and executed. This chapter will describe the necessary components associated with the practice of seeking a new position.

Presenting Your Credentials

The way you learn about the availability of a position determines how you apply for it. While the list is not exhaustive, here are some of the possibilities and recommended ways to respond.

In each of these instances, you need a current resume that has been written in a style most appropriate to the situation. The other thing that is essential in almost every case is a cover letter that personalizes the resume and conveys information not included in it.

Source	Response
Newspaper advertisement	Send a resume and cover letter, then follow their instructions—possibly completing their formal application.
Unsolicited inquiry.	Send your resume and a cover letter explaining your interest in the company. The alternative letter discussed later in this chapter is also a possibility.

(cont'd)

Source	Response
A recruiter contacted you.	Send your resume through the recruiter who has already developed contacts within the company. The recruiter will interview you and provide additional information focused on the position.
Posted announcement.	Follow the instructions and include a resume and cover letter.

RESUME COVER LETTERS

The cover letter has a mission as important as the resume itself—to get it into the hands of the right person and to motivate that person to read it. Here are some points to consider as you prepare your cover letter.

Question	Answer
To whom should the cover letter be addressed?	The hiring official, if at all possible. There are times when you must respect the protocol of sending it through personnel, but the objective is to place it in the hands of the person to whom you would report if hired.
How do I know who that is?	Inquire. Don't call and say you are an applicant. Do your homework and find out enough about the organization to identify the right person. Call the department and ask one of your potential co-workers. While you are at it, get the full name, spelling, and title correct.
How do I get their attention?	Make a statement or two that indicates you know something about the company and the position. Say how you learned about the vacancy.
How do I learn that?	Read newspapers, trade journals, business references in the library, call the public relations department of large firms for an annual report or recent news releases. Call the department and find a future peer willing to discuss the situation candidly. Call a competing firm and do the same.
What is your first priority for the cover letter?	To get your resume in the hands of the hiring official.
The next priority?	To get the hiring official's attention and impress him or her favorably enough to read your resume.

192

(cont'd)

Question	Answer
What would do that besides the company and position knowledge already mentioned?	Indicate how you can be of value to the company and the hiring official. How your skills and experience can solve a problem or contribute to company growth.
What is the ultimate objective of your cover letter?	To get an interview to state your case personally and have a chance at conveying the right chemistry, which only a personal interview can communicate.
What should the tone of the cover letter be?	Straightforward, positive, brief, in the language of the business in question—don't be overly obvious, but speak in terms meaningful to the hiring official.
How should the cover letter end?	Asking for an interview. Suggest a time when you will be in the area and offer to stop by, if convenient.
What other issues might be addressed in the cover letter?	Suggested times and places to reach you by telephone—whether or not a call to your office is okay. Whether or not your current employer is aware of your inquiry, or if confidentiality is required. Current compensation might be volunteered—only if requested or if there is concern about the adequacy of pay for the new position.
What about dropping names?	If there is a relevant common acquaintance who has agreed to be used as such a link, it can strengthen your letter. Be sure the reference is freely given and positive—enthusiastic is better.
Should I mention my reason for leaving?	It is not essential, but can clear the air on a point that is likely to require explanation eventually. Make it brief, general, and positive. If there is a serious problem that must be disclosed, do so as benignly as possible at this point and offer to elaborate at the interview.

Model Cover Letter

Wilson W. Woodruff
399 Calumet Avenue, Apartment 130
Washington, DC 20017
202-283-0099

January 22, 1990

Carson A. Howard
Head, Trust Investment Division
Holiday National Bank & Trust Company
892 Brickyard Parkway
Williamsburg, VA 24891

Dear Mr. Howard:

I am responding to your announcement in the January 21, 1990 edition of The Washington Post in which you sought applications for the position of Corporate Trust Investment Officer. Please consider this letter and the accompanying resume to be my application for that position.

As my resume relates in more detail, I have five years of successful corporate trust experience in the $750 million dollar department of Jones Bank & Trust in Washington. Our institutions serve a similar middle market clientele and I believe my contributions to your corporate calling effort in the Washington market could be quite attractive. Last year I increased funds under management by 43 percent and am well on the way to substantially increasing that performance this year.

John Samuels of your institution and I attended evening classes together while pursuing our MBAs. I have discussed the position with him and he has agreed to respond to any questions that you might have concerning my personal or professional qualities. I would welcome your discreet inquiries anywhere in the industry, but ask that you not contact my present employer until I am considered to be a serious candidate. At that point, I would make the appropriate announcement of my interest in your opportunity.

My tenure at Jones has been very positive and my goal in seeking this change is to achieve professional growth not available to me there. I hope that it will be possible for us to discuss our mutual interests personally in the near future. I will be in your area the week of February 7-10 and would be glad to stop by, if you would find that convenient. Please feel free to call me at the office or my residence if further information would be helpful.

Sincerely,

Wilson W. Woodruff

THE ALTERNATIVE LETTER

If you are sending out unsolicited resumes not directed toward a known vacancy, consider a combination letter and resume. These are one page long, addressed to a specific person with the potential to hire you, and contain enough information to highlight your accomplishments and tell why you would be qualified for a position in the organization. They have many of the characteristics of a Competency Cluster or Focused Resume.

Such letters are known variously as market letters, broadcast letters, confetti letters, and PAR (problem-action-result) letters, according to David Rottman, writing in a *National Business Employment Weekly* reprint (undated). The author says that a well-conceived letter of this type can draw a far higher response rate for unsolicited mailings than a traditional cover letter and resume. Twenty to thirty percent is possible for a good letter.

The objective is to get something brief and personally interesting into the hands of someone who can grant an interview if he or she likes the qualities you communicate in your one-pager. Rottman suggests that you begin with one of several lead-ins:

- Mention a mutual acquaintance who has the respect of the hiring official and would follow up with a strong reference if asked;

- Do some research and mention a quote or fact from a recent business publication that involves the target employer;

- List a personal accomplishment that has relevance for the person and company to whom you are writing; or

- Begin with something novel and creative—best left for those in creative career fields such as advertising.

After you have the person's attention, devote the core of your letter to establishing that you are qualified to do the job. Quantify what you have already done and then focus on what you would be doing for them. Close with a request for an interview, as in any cover letter.

Sample Market Letter

Maria E. Forbes
3497 Grant Street
Pittsburgh, PA 15234
412-261-9987

January 24, 1990

Clyde J. Hoover
Dean of Alumni Affairs
University of Eastern California
700 Palm Drive
Eighty-Nine Palms, CA 00784

Dear Dean Hoover:

I enjoyed your presentation at the December meeting of the National Alumni Administrators' Association at Atlantic City. The insights you provided on the prospects for increasing alumni participation by the use of up-scale travel and credit card programs were of particular interest to me.

In five years of service as Director of Alumni Membership at Concord College, I have increased participation by 120 percent. Much of that success accrues to smaller scale versions of the kinds of promotional programs that you advocate.

Other professional accomplishments that might interest you are:

- Initiated the first statewide alumni rental car discount program in Pennsylvania;
- Successfully petitioned the state lottery for college alumni program development funding;
- Increased alumni volunteer participation by 200 percent.

I would welcome the opportunity to discuss the possiblity of my joining your staff at the end of the current academic year. Since I will be in California on February 21st, I will call your office to see if a brief personal visit might be possible on the morning of the 22nd.

Sincerely,

Maria E. Forbes

Richard Davis, writing in *Continuing Education Today* (1989), describes a similar approach that he calls a Notice of Availability. Instead of a letter format, he suggests a one-page outline consisting of headings and information similar to these:

Letterhead

Date

Notice of Availability (Your job title)

Position Desired (Job title)

Salary Required (Negotiable)

Available (Date)

Qualifications (In summary form)

Current Position (Job title)

Special Skills

References/Resume Available Upon Request

Recommended Contact Request (Recipient provides this if he or she knows
of someone looking for a person with the sender's qualifications)

Thank You

Davis suggests that response rates for mailings based on names and addresses taken from current professional directories have been in the fifteen percent range. He found that most resulted in leads for excellent positions not seen advertised elsewhere.

Sample Notice of Availability

Maria E. Forbes
3497 Grant Street
Pittsburgh, PA 15234
412-261-9987

January 24, 1990

ANNOUNCEMENT OF AVAILABILITY

Creative, Enthusiastic College Alumni Director

POSITION DESIRED: Director or Assistant Director of Alumni Affairs.

SALARY REQUIRED: Negotiable above mid-thirties.

AVAILABLE: August 1990

QUALIFICATIONS: Master's Degree in Marketing
Five years experience as Alumni Membership Director
Two years as Alumni Publications Coordinator
Three years as Student Services Officer
Numerous professional publications
Alumni event planning
Alumni membership drive coordination
Secretary, National Alumni Professionals Association
Proposal writing
Private giving experience

CURRENT POSITION: Associate Alumni Program Coordinator
Concord College, PA

SPECIAL SKILLS: Computer mailing list preparation and maintenance.

REFERENCES AND RESUME AVAILABLE UPON REQUEST

SUGGESTED CONTACT: If you have or know of a position available, please
complete the information below and return it to me.

Position Available: _____
Contact Person: _____
Title: _____
Address: _____
Telephone: _____

THANK YOU

Interviewing

After the cover letter and resume have succeeded, it is time to go face to face—maybe voice to voice will come first, in the form of a telephone interview. Here are some considerations that will help you to make the most of this crucial opportunity.

- Know something about the company, the job, and the person doing the interviewing. You do not have to pretend to be an expert, just show awareness of at least the basics:

  What is the business of the company?

  Is it relatively new or long established?

  What kind of customers does it serve?

  What does it produce?

  What is your interviewer's position?

  Outstanding acomplishments, reputation, etc. for either the company or the interviewer?

- Dress for the occasion. Standard business wardrobe is easy to define and replicate. Unless you are absolutely certain that something less will do, dress as you would for a business meeting with a top client. Clothes clean and pressed, shoes shined—no rundown heels, etc.

- Be on time. Not very early—never late.

- Come alone. Let the emphasis properly be on you, not the spouse and kids or whoever might have made the trip.

- Make a dry run on the location, if practical, to know where to park and generally solve any problems that might make you late or flustered the day of the interview.

- No gum chewing, smoking, obvious perfume, aftershave, excesses of makeup, fashion, or anything else that might detract from your bearing.

- Have flexible arrangements—no parking meter to feed, no early flight that must be met, and never another interview that you must get to right after this one.

- Be relaxed, but not familiar. Let any informality be insisted upon by the interviewer—first names, removing jackets, etc.

- Respond freely, but do not volunteer information not requested if it has any potential for embarrassment.

- Be ready for the standard questions—Why do you want the job? Why do you feel qualified? Where do you see yourself professionally in five years? What can you do for the company? Are you willing to travel and relocate? What kinds of people do you get along with best? . . . least well? What do you like to read? Book last read? Your strong points and weaknesses?

Your greatest accomplishments and failures? Tell me about your personality. How did you like your boss? Do you have any problems we should be aware of that would affect your performance in this position? Why should we hire you? When could you begin? Why are you leaving your present job? Why do you want to work for this company? What is your minimum acceptable salary? What would you like to ask me?

- Stay honest in answering these and other questions, but understand that you are being tested. Do not close doors with absolute responses. Try to put a positive spin on anything you can and suggest that there is room to negotiate almost anything. Salary questions should wait until an offer is made other than to say what you presently earn, that you expect to make more, and that the advertised range would appear to accommodate that need. Do not get put into a position of being negative or getting mad. How you respond may be as important as what you say.

- Watch for clues that it is time to end the session. Do not persist with questions or explanations beyond the point indicated by the interviewer's body language and other signs that enough has been said.

- Have a neatly typed list of your references' names, addresses and telephone numbers in case they are requested. It is assumed that you have informed them of the interview and the possibility that they will be contacted.

FOLLOW-THROUGH

When the interview ends, be ready with a comfortable handshake, a smile, and an expression of appreciation for the opportunity to discuss the position. You should also say that you have continuing interest in the position. After you have returned home, send a brief letter of thanks for the courtesies extended by the employer during the interview, include any additional information that you may have agreed to send, and, again, express your interest in being the person hired. Offer to clarify questions that may arise, provide further references that might be required, and furnish any other information that would be helpful.

With those things done, there is nothing to be gained by making further inquiries about the status of your application. After the interview and the follow-up courtesies, be responsive to any contact that might be made. If something materially changes in your situation, make the employer aware of it. Otherwise, the ball is in his court and you can only diminish your stature by seeming overly anxious. That does not preclude a businesslike check of your status if it has been an unduly long time or if you must decide on accepting another offer.

The Hiring Process

You need to understand the hiring process in order to participate in it most effectively. By knowing what to expect and having a realistic perspective, you will be spared some potential frustration and improve the odds of ending up with the position you want.

THE HIRING CYCLE

After your initial application, your resume and supporting materials are screened along with others and, if interest persists, you are called for a telephone interview. If that goes well, a personal interview is arranged. Depending on the firm, you may speak initially with a human resources specialist (personnel officer) who will confirm that you meet the major job qualifications, appear genuinely interested in the position, and seem to have the standards of warmth, personality, and professional image that the company seeks.

A word about salary. The company will want to confirm that it can afford your services. This is an initial, general inquiry and not a negotiation of salary. Unless you are clearly out of range, the hiring process will go forward. Do your best to leave the salary question open until late in the game when the employer has developed a strong interest in you. An appropriate response early in the screening is that you are presently making $—— and that you would be expecting a reasonable incentive above that to justify the move. Leave it at that, if you can. A realistic expectation for a salary increase when changing jobs is the ten to fifteen percent range—sometimes fifteen to twenty percent, rarely more. If that is inconsistent with what you feel you must have, you need to review the entire situation. While you might enjoy some unique status that commands more, serious differences in expectations should be resolved early. Use your grapevine or, if necessary, directly determine early on that your goal is achievable. Unless realistic compromise is potentially possible, the prospects of your ultimately being hired become small.

This may take awhile. Timing between the cycles of the hiring process can vary widely and you must be prepared for some emotional ups and downs. Rarely is your application followed immediately by the employer's call, a personal interview, and an offer. It more often goes like this—

- You get reasonably enthusiastic about the prospect of something new and better. If you have been encouraged to apply, it is a compliment—your value in the marketplace is reaffirmed.

- A week or more goes by and no call—due to a number of good reasons that usually have nothing to do with how the employer feels about you. A key person got sick, had to take a trip, or had to deal with an unexpected development. Someone decided that they must all await the results of another ad. A decision was made to interview several local candidates first . . . and so on.

- Such delays can work on your morale and attitude. Initial enthusiasm can turn to posturing to avoid rejection— "I didn't really want it anyway. . . ."

- That kind of thinking is usually unfounded and unnecessary. Rarely is the delay anything more than a large organization trying to fit something that it doesn't do everyday—hiring—into what it must do every day—deal with the business at hand and unexpected problems totally unrelated to your hiring.

- Be patient. Everything that was true on your most enthusiastic day probably still is. Well-founded personal and professional reasons attracted you to the position in the first place. Chances are they included a mix of opportunity, geography, and compensation. That is all still true and you have nothing to lose by seeing it through—possibly much to gain.

Your attitude means a lot. Whether you are competing for a CEO's position or something less, the company is trying to select the very best and will make the effort necessary to have an outstanding group from which to choose. You are well prepared or you would not have reached the point of serious consideration.

After the objective criteria have been satisfied, the selection process narrows to more subjective things. It is very important that you be yourself and do not attempt to play a role that you think will be popular. You have to come up with and maintain an honest, positive attitude that conveys something like this:

> "Yes, this sounds like an opportunity that could really be of interest to me—I want to learn more about it and help you understand just how I could become a very fine addition to your organization."

You will experience ups and downs in your enthusiasm for the position. Ask the necessary questions to resolve your concerns, but keep your positive interest apparent throughout. You are always in a position to say no to an offer. You are rarely able to revive interest once you have turned interviewers off with an attitude with which they are not prepared to deal. Keep it positive and keep their interest growing. Final negotiations are best handled at the end when you are in the strongest position—they have selected you and made an offer. They want to see it work at that point and will be more apt to satisfy some concerns that you might have—assuming there are no big surprises that alter basic expectations that have been building from the beginning.

Impressions matter. When all is said and done and the final selection is made, you will have left impressions with a number of people. Good impressions can make you the winner in a group of relative equals. Consider how the following impressions can work for you:

- Quiet confidence and a good-natured interest in the company and future co-workers, consistently and naturally displayed with more than one person in a variety of settings.

- A general tone of openness and warmth. Say a genuine thank you to the person who helped arrange your visit, send brief, positive letters of appreciation following interviews. Express your continuing interest. Employers want to feel comfortable with you and expect that their clients will feel the same.

- Display of poise and equanimity, not overwhelmed by a single disappointment. Issues calmly resolved in a mutually satisfactory way.

- No up-front demands. Made sure that differences were potentially resolvable, but left their resolution for the proper point in the hiring process—at the offer stage.

- Had some things to offer for the good of the organization with an honest interest in accomplishing them.

- Positive attitude. Made no negative comments about past associations—even if warranted.

- Clean, crisp, well-groomed business image—traditional business wardrobe, obviously cleaned and pressed—the kind of person employers want representing their firm.

Employer fears. There is considerable risk, expense, and trauma for a hiring organization. It would like to avoid going through the same hiring demands again in the near future. You must be honest and genuine, but do not go in saying that you plan on leaving in two years. Before your interview, formulate a solid and positive career plan that shows your commitment to the organization will be long-term in nature—more than five years. Reality may dictate otherwise, but your incoming goal should be one with which the employer can be comfortable.

Finally, the counteroffer/buy-back. The hiring cycle has been completed successfully, an offer has been made and accepted. Is it over? Maybe not. What remains is for you tell your present employer. It is not uncommon for employers to make an unexpectedly good offer in order to retain you. Such counteroffers are usually for the purpose of buying them time to replace you. Why did it take your resignation to make you so valuable to the company? Were you only leaving because of a change in pay or some alteration of your duties—or were there larger reasons? If so, it is doubtful that the counteroffer will change your mind about leaving. Think this all through and have your answer ready well before the emotional moment of actual resignation. Buy-backs are seldom still in their jobs a year later. Decide whether or not you really want to move on. If the answer is yes and the opportunity presents itself, be prepared to follow through without anguishing over the final step.

5 COMPUTERS, FAX, AND VIDEOTAPE

Technology can enhance your resume and support your job-seeking efforts. Nothing is a substitute for valid resume content and a well-executed job search, but modern electronic enhancements could conceivably provide you with the winning edge when the competition gets tight. What follows is new thinking in the field of resume crafting and presentation. It represents the exception and not the rule. Spend your primary effort on the preparation of the finest resume and cover letter possible—but be aware of the potential of computers, fax, and videotape.

Computers

Word processing is at the heart of modern resume preparation. A typewriter will do, but anyone with access to a personal computer and first-rate word-processing software has a clear advantage. Add to the arsenal a laser or high-quality ink-jet printer and you have a formidable resume preparation arrangement.

COMPUTERS AND RESUMES IN GENERAL

The computer gives you more than just a fancy final product. It is crucial to keeping your information current and accurate. By altering several elements of your basic resume, you can produce an endless variety of truly personalized editions. The need for printing a quantity of soon obsolete resumes ends with the ability to print an up-to-the minute one instantly.

If you neither own a personal computer with the qualities described nor have access to one at work, consider the rental option. Most cities now have walk-in shops where you pay an hourly rate for the use of a thoroughly modern computer system fully capable of producing a great resume. They will show you how to use it and sell you a disk on which to keep your resume and supporting correspondence for future use.

It is really quite simple to master a few techniques such as centering, bold-facing, italicizing, and selecting interesting type faces that will add immeasurably to the professional appearance of your resume. Printing it on a laser printer is no challenge whatsoever. The whole exercise will cost you far less than you imagine and it gets cheaper after you learn how to use the equipment efficiently.

All of the advantages just described for resume preparation apply to the support areas surrounding your job search as well. Correspondence is easily prepared and stored for later modification and use in future efforts. Lists of references can be maintained efficiently and customized lists put together to suit changing requirements. A record of your job search activities, company points of contact, and names, addresses, and telephone numbers are readily kept in the computer.

Your ability to use a computer is an invaluable skill. Rarely is a job interview conducted today that does not raise the question of computer literacy. It is not difficult to be able to answer with a confident "yes," and the preparation of your own resume is a great way to begin gaining the necessary skills. Friends and acquaintances who have conquered the basics of using a computer will fall all over themselves to show you how—let them. It is a great convenience and a real business necessity in the modern office.

SPECIFIC COMPUTER TECHNIQUES FOR RESUME WRITERS

- **Typing:** With the computer you gain complete flexibility to let your ideas flow, knowing you can alter, delete, cut and paste, and change things endlessly until you get it right—and right can vary with the recipient.

- **Proofing:** Most word-processing programs have spell checkers that will save you the embarrassment of most typos as well as misspelled words. Some programs will even suggest things that you might reconsider grammatically.

- **Aesthetics:** When you get beyond the fundamentals of saying the right thing with the correctly chosen and spelled words, much of the impact of your resume will depend on how it is arranged and presented. The computer extends the flexibility you enjoy in typing to viewing your resume as a whole. Depending on your equipment and software, that might mean printing copies and revising them several times, or just summoning the preview feature of your system to see if you find it pleasing before going to the printer.

While computers and printers vary in their capabilities, it does not require desktop publishing skills or software to use the following techniques:

TYPE STYLE AND LAYOUT

Variety and emphasis can be added by changing the size and characteristics of what you type. Here are some examples of how you can add interest and direct the reader's attention by altering type style and its arrangement.

Plain left-justified courier type is clean and okay.

```
Kent L. Schwartz
3595 Congress Avenue, NW
Washington, DC 20033
202-991-0245
```

Centering it makes it a little more interesting.

```
                Kent L. Schwartz
             3595 Congress Avenue, NW
               Washington, DC 20033
                 202-991-0245
```

You can stress the most important part by making it larger and reducing the size of a minor item like the telephone number.

```
                Kent L. Schwartz
             3595 Congress Avenue, NW
               Washington, DC 20033
                 202-991-0245
```

Boldfacing can add even more emphasis.

```
               Kent L. Schwartz
             3595 Congress Avenue, NW
               Washington, DC 20033
                 202-991-0245
```

The final touch might be the selection of a typeface that suits your image. (These are just a few examples—what is actually available will vary depending on your computer and supporting software.)

Kent L. Schwartz
3595 Congress Avenue, NW
Washington, DC 20033
202-991-0245

Kent L. Schwartz
3595 Congress Avenue, NW
Washington, DC 20033
202-991-0245

Kent L. Schwartz
3595 Congress Avenue, NW
Washington, DC 20033
202-991-0245

Kent L. Schwartz
3595 Congress Avenue, NW
Washington, DC 20033
202-991-0245

Kent L. Schwartz
3595 Congress Avenue, NW
Washington, DC 20033
202-991-0245

Kent L. Schwartz
3595 Congress Avenue, NW
Washington, DC 20033
202-991-0245

Even more variety is possible on systems that also let you italicize, outline, shadow, and underline (clockwise, beginning upper left)—capabilities that are not at all uncommon on today's personal computers.

Kent L. Schwartz
3595 Congress Avenue, NW
Washington, DC 20033
202-991-0245

Kent L. Schwartz
3595 Congress Avenue, NW
Washington, DC 20033
202-991-0245

Kent L. Schwartz
3595 Congress Avenue, NW
Washington, DC 20033
202-991-0245

Kent L. Schwartz
3595 Congress Avenue, NW
Washington, DC 20033
202-991-0245

The use of all of these variations is dictated by good taste and aesthetic balance. A traditional business resume would probably not get into the use of outline or shadow type. Boldfacing would have a place, as would underlining and italicizing. The latter might be more appropriate in the body of the resume where you strive to distinguish between job title and employer, for example. When in doubt, simplify. Do not succumb to the rapture of your computer and produce a resume that is so dominated by style variations that the reader is drawn away from the points you want to emphasize. If there is no item of information worthy of emphasis—or if the technique you have chosen fails to impart that emphasis pleasantly—forget it.

Typeface variations are not the only consideration in preparing a resume on your computer. Many popular word-processing software packages give you the means to arrange side-by-side paragraphs. They can be very useful in placing eye-catching headers with elaborating details next to them. Here is an example:

Skills	• Speech preparation
	• News release writing
	• Media event coordination
	• Publication creation
	• Articulation of institutional image
Accomplishments	• Increased alumni participation by 23 percent during two year directorship.
	• Won the State Education Associations' Promotion of the Year Award for 1985.
	• Collection of my drafted speeches published as a nationally distributed monograph.

Remember that many computers provide bullets (•) or check marks (√) to add clarity to your lists of attributes. There are trademark (™), copyright (©) and registered (®) symbols that could add professionalism to a specialized resume. The same is true of scientific and language symbols. Avoid the contrived use of any of these techniques, but be aware of their potential when the situation calls for them.

Another advantage of computerized resumes is the option of reducing the size of the final version. If you have everything perfectly expressed and arranged, but find that it overflows to the next page by several lines, it is easy to reduce the type size by one setting and make it fit. Another approach is to print with a percentage reduction (e.g., when you select the print option you can elect to make it ninety percent of the actual size, etc.) that places your full resume on a page neatly without noticeable loss.

Cutting and pasting is computer terminology for electronically selecting and removing certain passages and inserting them somewhere else. On a lesser scale, inserting and spreading text is another means of flexibility not found on typewriters. With it you enter a word, sentence, paragraph, or document at any point and add text—the computer pushes the rest of the text forward and accommodates your changes. The reverse is true for deleting material.

Paragraphs can be treated with the balance and style previously only available from a print shop. Here are a few things that you can do conveniently on a personal computer.

Centering

BEFORE
Strong organizational and people skills. Proven leader with over 6 years of progressively successful experience in personnel, management, and sales. Seek to combine talents at senior management level as administrative assistant with potential for assuming broader responsibilities.

AFTER
Strong organizational and people skills. Proven leader with over 6 years of progressively successful experience in personnel, management, and sales. Seek to combine talents at senior management level as administrative assistant with potential for assuming broader responsibilities.

Justified Type

BEFORE
Strong organizational and people skills. Proven leader with over 6 years of progressively successful experience in personnel, management, and sales. Seek to combine talents at senior management level as administrative assistant with potential for assuming broader responsibilities.

AFTER
Strong organizational and people skills. Proven leader with over 6 years of progressively successful experience in personnel, management, and sales. Seek to combine talents at senior management level as administrative assistant with potential for assuming broader responsibilities.

Inset Margins

BEFORE
Strong organizational and people skills. Proven leader with over 6 years of progressively successful experience in personnel, management, and sales. Seek to

combine talents at senior management level as administrative assistant with potential for assuming broader responsibilities.

AFTER

>   Strong organizational and people skills. Proven leader with over 6 years of progressively successful experience in personnel, management, and sales. Seek to combine talents at senior management level as administrative assistant with potential for assuming broader responsibilities.

Hanging Indents

BEFORE

• Strong organizational and people skills. Proven leader with over 6 years of progressively successful experience in personnel, management, and sales. Seek to combine talents at senior management level as administrative assistant with potential for assuming broader responsibilities.

AFTER

• Strong organizational and people skills. Proven leader with over 6 years of progressively successful experience in personnel, management, and sales. Seek to combine talents at senior management level as administrative assistant with potential
  for assuming broader responsibilities.

BOILERPLATE

Personalization is one of the computer's strongest capabilities for the resume writer. While it can be a disaster if you leave John Jones's personal data in the resume that you are sending to Frank Smith, the advantages are worth the extra diligence required to get it right.

If you are a person whose talents might be applied in several contexts, you can have a basic resume in which you insert special paragraphs denoting the emphasis appropriate for each. One may stress your portfolio management skills for job-seeking as an in-house money manager. Another might put the emphasis on your business development accomplishments, if the position calls for someone with strong marketing skills. Customized clauses and paragraphs, carefully used, can accomplish this degree of personalization.

Resumes can effortlessly be directed toward a specific person and position, if appropriate. Here is an example of how that might be done:

Marsha K. Grant
21 South Market Place
North Laguna, CA 96731
704-223-0977

Resume Prepared for the Consideration of:
Carlton M. Donnaly
Human Resources Manager
The Wilcoxon Companies

Director of Marketing Position

With such a beginning, a resume can be directed toward a succession of specific employers, each one giving the appearance of a customized document prepared for that person. Even for those jaded enough to know it is done with ease on a personal computer, this adds a nice touch and shows effort that speaks well for your interest, thoroughness, and initiative.

SOFTWARE

Finally, the software itself (together with computer hardware that supports it) is what gives you the capabilities just discussed. There is a vast marketplace filled with products of varying costs and complexity that will work nicely in resume preparation. As you shop for a specific word-processing package, one thing you might consider is whether it has commercially prepared resume *templates* available. With templates you have an already formatted outline for various styles of resumes. You simply enter your own specific data. Depending on your level of interest and creativity, this may or may not be helpful. Such templates work in conjunction with specific word-processing programs. Local software or computer stores can assist you in putting together an effective combination of products. Computer magazines are filled with articles and advertising that discuss such things. They also contain advertising for firms that sell software by mail.

Fax

Facsimile transmission really is not anything new. News services have relied on it for decades. The newness is how very common the fax has become. Today it can be found in nearly every business of any consequence. The machines are easy to use and priced for the consumer at under a thousand dollars. If you do not have personal access to one, fax services are available for a reasonable fee at copy centers, mail box and packaging stores, and other retail service businesses. Typical charges are several dollars per page transmitted or received.

What this means to the job applicant is a tremendous capacity for instant response to a hiring notice or a hiring official's request for additional information. A fax has the impact of a telegram. It certainly gets treated with more urgency than the incoming mail. Use that to your advantage both to meet urgent deadlines and as a device for standing out in the crowd of incoming resumes.

Since the quality of most fax machines leaves something to be desired, you should use a cover sheet indicating that a printed copy of your resume will follow in the mail. Properly done, the use of the fax to introduce yourself to an employer shows several desirable qualities:

- genuinely prompt reaction to deadlines or requests for information;

- familiarity with the latest in business technology; and

- a competitive quality translated into the business environment that precedes you and gives you a distinctiveness not shared by the average applicant.

It goes without saying that the fax will do nothing to enhance an otherwise unattractive resume. The advantage comes when you have something special to offer the employer and you add to that basic advantage by reacting with the speed and impact of a fax.

The same advantage can be used in all correspondence surrounding the hiring process. You can make an arrangement with a local fax service to call you when something is received in your name. They are happy to have you use their fax number as though it were your own. The charge is minimal for the impact of telling a hired official that they can fax the application or job description or company benefits brochure, or whatever, to you.

Another potential use is to provide immediate letters of reference. Most of your reference sources will have fax machines in their offices and would be glad to transmit their recommendations. It has the advantage of great promptness and says something about how you do business with others—if they care enough about you and you were sharp enough to arrange for a faxed reference, it cannot help but reflect favorably.

Anything can be overdone or done poorly. Be cautious about using the fax approach to resume delivery and support. Save it for when it might really have a place—a tight deadline, an urgent request for follow-up information, or a quick reference that might close a deal before the enthusiasm of the moment cools. If you add a commercial fax number to your resume for impact, be sure to check the service regularly and make certain that an important communication to you doesn't sit uncollected.

Videotape

The latest resume-service marketing device is adding a videotaped interview to basic resume preparation. The idea clearly has potential. One company claims to conduct a professional interview with the candidate and then make that tape available to employers seeking his or her skills. The advantages for both the employer and candidate are potentially great, if the process is handled well by all concerned.

The similarity of this approach to video dating services is apparent, as is the potential for abuse or costly ineffectiveness. If you find yourself in an area served by a video resume service, it may represent an interesting opportunity to present your talents in a uniquely effective way. You will have to judge the soundness of the particular company offering the service. References from both the candidate and the employer side of the hiring equation would be a reasonable place to begin in evaluating the potential effectiveness of such a firm. Readers should exercise the same level of consumer awareness that they would in selecting any important service.

In a totally independent vein, it would be entirely possible to arrange for the production of a short personal video with a professional studio. You could write the script for a video resume and distribute copies to selected employers around the country, perhaps after their favorable response to your printed resume or market letter. It might advance your prospects in a situation where your paper resume and telephone interview are sufficiently promising to warrant a look at you on the VCR, but not a trip across the country. If the tape conveys the qualities sought, the actual interview could follow.

A video tape definitely adds to the impression gained from the resume and a telephone conversation. Everyone has access to a VCR player, so there would be no difficulty reviewing your tape if the employer was interested. There is a good chance that the hiring official will be curious enough to ask for and look at the tape. You might even find that you have his personal attention at home after business hours. Hand-held home video cameras are not apt to convey the impression you want. Expect to spend some time and money on a quality studio production, if you decide to follow this approach.

6

SPECIAL SITUATIONS

A special resume may be called for to address the particular needs of job seekers who approach the world of work from nontraditional situations. The normal expectation of an employer advertising a vacancy is to attract people who are working full time in a job logically aligned with the position being offered. The person applying for a senior management position is usually someone doing well as a middle manager in roughly the same kind of setting as that of the prospective new employer.

When the expected pattern is broken, the approach to resume writing needs special attention. The final product is not that different, but negative things are anticipated and neutralized by properly drafting and presenting the resume. Strengths can be accentuated that actually make the nontraditional worker more attractive than those with patterns of ideal career progression.

Among those who will find this chapter particularly useful are individuals who are:

- *returning to the workplace following an absence* caused by family obligations, a small business venture, involuntary loss of employment, or full-time study;

- *making work-study arrangements* as a lead-in to a career position;

- *establishing a second career* following an early retirement;

- *looking for flexibility* in working hours or overall arrangements; or

- *coming from other countries and cultures* and struggling to articulate the value of their work and training in alien settings.

215

Returning to the Workplace

Stepping out of the lock-step career path is increasingly common. Many reasons account for breaks in the entry-level to mid-level to senior-level march through the ranks that is sometimes expected. A free society provides opportunities for uniquely personalized work lives and many Americans exercise the options. Another factor is that our rapidly evolving, competitive economy does not necessarily guarantee job continuity throughout a lifetime.

While the possibilities go beyond the examples, here are some reasons why you might find yourself preparing a resume explaining why you are coming to the job market with a less than traditional work history:

- A period of unemployment, self-employment, or part-time employment for the purpose of raising a family;

- A small business or consulting venture of your own that is no longer as attractive as a traditional position;

- A merger or other organizational quirk that leaves you on the outside looking in; or

- A period of full-time study was necessary to change careers or achieve a desired level of employment.

RECOMMENDED APPROACH

In each of these instances the resume, cover letter, and your general approach to the potential employer is one of positive objectivity. You do not attempt to mask your true situation, neither do you apologize for it. Determine what your marketable strengths are and decide how to bring them to the attention of someone who can use them.

You are what you are—there is no need for, or anything to be gained by, posturing as something else. If you are a homemaker who only worked briefly as a management trainee before spending ten years outside the workplace, then you are an entry-level employee with some experience—PLUS a great deal of added maturity and motivation with which to make the best of your remaining career.

There are ways to deal with the apparent negatives of your situation. The following table lists a few of the things you might face (overtly or beneath the surface) and how to compensate:

Challenge	Response
Your experience is out of date.	I have remained active in the marketplace as a consumer of your services and can bring that valued perspective to the job.

(cont'd)

Challenge	Response
You are too old for this level position.	Think, act, and look young—this is usually more a problem of perception than reality. Chronological age has little to do with working age in most contemporary, non-physically demanding jobs.
Your education is dated.	Take a refresher course or seminar. It will not only bring you up to date on terminology, but you stand a good chance of networking with people who can help you find employment.

RESUME TIPS

Since you lack the perfect continuity that looks best in a Work History Resume, opt for the Competency Cluster or Focused Resume that places the emphasis on what you can do, rather than where and for how long you have done it. Market yourself very deliberately. Do your homework on the company and the job being offered. Put yourself in the hiring official's shoes and make a case for why you should be an attractive hire.

Avoid gimmicks, but take advantage of couching your experience in terms and examples that relate to the situation. If you are listing experience as a telephone volunteer for your alumni association fund drive or the local public television station, speak in terms of telemarketing. Use the OVERVIEW part of the resume to portray yourself as someone

- aware of what the position entails;
- qualified to perform the duties; and
- motivated to assume a realistic role in the company.

Before the hiring official ever becomes embroiled in your precise experience and training, you want to have made the point that you know what she or he wants and can make a convincing case for being able to provide it.

Next comes the selection of competency clusters or qualifications and achievements that will substantiate your claim. This is where your homework pays off—by knowing what the situation actually entails, you have the advantage of being able to translate your attributes into those valued by the employer. The same experience can be stated in general terms or reasonably job-specific terms—the latter will tend to focus employer attention on exactly what you can do for him, rather than tasking him with reaching the same conclusion the hard way—by puzzling over a less deliberately arranged resume.

Comments can be used as a closing reaffirmation that you understand the realities of the employer's needs and can meet them. You can tersely answer the obvious questions that might be associated with your situation and put them to rest—at least until the interview. These are only examples:

These and similar brief comments can become subtle building blocks of confidence

Question	Answer
Why did you leave your last job?	The company was recently bought by XYA Corporation and thirty accounting positions were consolidated into ten at XYA's West Coast offices.
Why did you close your business or consulting practice?	After five years of successfully building my company, it was acquired by the ABC Company. I am intrigued by the opportunity your vacancy represents.
With your background, what appreciation could you possibly have for our career development expectations?	I am currently enrolled in the CFA study group and plan to sit for the Series I examination in June.

between you and the reader of your resume. Throw out as many little lifelines as you can that will give them honest cause to reel you in for a closer look. The employer wants to sense that you understand his needs, can meet them, and have the potential for fitting in and growing. A traditional work history is not the only way to go about establishing such a link between applicant and employer—you just might have to work a little harder at the logic of the presentation if you lack the step-by-step progression of readily understood and expected jobs.

Work-Study Arrangements

There is no more certain way to get the job you want after graduation than having an already established working relationship with the target company as a highly regarded student-worker. Summer and part-time jobs are the link to career positions for thousands of students every year. There are approaches to resume preparation that can help the aspirants achieve this goal.

RECOMMENDED APPROACH

As a student applying for a part-time position with an organization, the best way to make your resume and cover letter stand out is to show evidence of career thinking. Convey that you are highly interested in the seasonal position for which you are applying, but aware of the opportunity's implications for overall career development.

This has to be done without overkill. The desired tone is that of someone aware of his present place in the order of things, but equally cognizant of where the career path leads. That is done by expressing interest in both the position and the company. Your cover letter is a good place to communicate awareness of what the firm does and its position in the marketplace. Remember to use a moderate tone and not to phrase your letter like a report. It is easy enough to check the business reference section of your library and learn the basic demographics on

Desired Message	Method of Relating It
I want this seasonal job—it is important to me for several reasons.	I value the work ethic and financial responsibility—this job will help me gain valuable work experience and avoid building debt as a student.
My education can contribute to doing this job well.	As a student of (engineering, marketing, or whatever) I have seen a lot of theory and case study examples of what you do at XYZ Corporation. That would bring me to the job with a lot of orientation already in place, anxious to apply it as a worker.
I can see future possibilities with XYZ Corporation.	I have a lot of respect for the market position of XYZ, have heard positive things about it as a place to build a career, and would welcome the opportunity for us to learn to know each other better in a worker-employer relationship.

the company with which you are communicating. Brief mention of a recent acquisition or new product is an appropriate way to note that you have some current awareness of the business world in general and your target company in particular.

RESUME TIPS

It is unlikely that you, as a student, have a chronology of employment that would warrant using the Work History Resume format. You are primarily interested in packaging your abilities, achievements, and strengths for the purpose of appealing to a certain kind of situation. The best resumes for that objective are the Competency Cluster and Focused Resume formats.

The OVERVIEW can be used to accomplish the following objectives:

- name the seasonal position you seek;

- qualify yourself for performing the required duties; and

- show possible career motivation.

All of this has to be done in several sentences. The statements merely need to convey that you know what the job entails, can (and, without saying so, are willing to) perform the work necessary, and that you have an interest that goes beyond this position after you finish your studies. Leave it to the body of the resume to actually develop and substantiate your OVERVIEW. It might read something like this:

OVERVIEW: Third-year electrical engineering student applying for the summer position as Field Engineering Aide III. Studies and prior Army experience qualify me for the testing environment. Concurrent objective of exploring future professional affiliation with XYZ Corp.

If you find it desirable to tie your resume presentation together with a concluding statement, the COMMENTS section can be added for that purpose. It is not the place to relate what has already been established, but it can be useful to focus everything on the particular objective and dispel any anticipated problems.

Question	Answer
Why are you still a student at the age of twenty-eight?	Describe your military service as relevant to your career—possibly a year spent touring Europe after leaving the service and prior to returning to college.
Why would you within a year of being a graduate engineer want a job like this?	Amplify your respect for learning the business from the inside out—this position could give you that perspective before crossing over to the professional level.
What kind of career expectations do you have?	If your awareness is sufficiently specific, briefly conclude with an expression of interest in exploring future employment with them in fiber optics transmission or whatever.

Establishing Second Careers

Government and industry both use the practice of offering early retirement to reduce their work force in a nondestructive way. People leave careers still vigorous enough to want the continued ritual of the workplace—the reason for getting out of bed in the morning, socialization with coworkers, the satisfaction of accomplishing something, and—last, but not necessarily least—money. Whether you are a military officer retired with a substantial pension in your mid-forties, or an older clerical worker relieved with a modest income by a large corporation, you may find yourself attempting to market your employment skills with a resume.

RECOMMENDED APPROACH

As a person with one career behind you, your objective is to look ahead to the next with a combination of experiences past and challenges desired. You are making a transition and trying to make the case that you have something to offer in the world of the new employer. Here are some of the attitudes that you may want to anticipate addressing with some subtlety in your resume and cover letter.

Attitude	Response
You are retired—why would I want to hire you?	In the modern workplace careers are sometimes incremental—retirement is often a misnomer for a person successfully transiting to another career stage.
Your background is from an entirely different work environment—how will you adapt to our situation?	Work is far more appropriately categorized by task than employer—I have successfully managed people and resouces for the last X years and I can do it for you.
What if you are looking to retire on the job?—my job!	The work ethic is very much a habit. My motivation for applying for this position is to continue deriving the satisfaction of a job well done—my references will vouch for my level of energy and commitment.

RESUME TIPS

The person pursuing a second career has a full choice of resume formats. If the position being sought is a logical extension of the career path that led to early retirement, the Work History Resume may very well be appropriate. If there is to be a substantial change of career direction, the better bet might be the Competency Cluster or Focused Resume format where prior experience can be translated into skills gained and achievements made.

Regardless of resume format, an appropriate OVERVIEW can be helpful in immediately establishing several basics:

- identify the position or category of position sought;

- mention your general qualifications for the job; and

- express some sincere motivation to pursue it.

While the points made will vary by job and background, here is an example of how you might begin:

OVERVIEW: Retired Navy senior enlisted woman with successful paramedical career seeks affiliation with a civilian health management organization. Fully certified professional anxious to continue rewarding health services career without interruption.

The body of the resume is then used to demonstrate that your claims to competency and experience are valid.

A concluding COMMENTS section can be helpful if you feel there is anything that would benefit from further interpretation. Although it must be kept brief, several sentences can tie together the several points that make your case for career continuity. Here are samples of issues that might be laid to rest with an appropriate comment:

Question	Answer
How do I as an employer in the X business compare the certification of a specialist who has spent an entire career working in Y?	Professional certification for paraprofessionals in military health care facilities is the same as for those in civilian hospitals.
How will a person accustomed to having military rank and authority function in the less structured civilian environment?	Express your authority and rank functionally with examples of responsibility, rather than power and rank—that will be more readily understood in the civilian sector.
You are still in Japan, how can I be assured you will be able to report for duty on the date you promise?	Mention that your retirement orders have been issued and that you will be separated from the service on a date comfortably in advance of your reporting date for the new position.

Looking for Flexibility

People find themselves wanting to be employed in the regular work force, but with less than a full-time schedule and, perhaps, at irregular hours. To their surprise, the same requirement often exists on the hiring side of the equation—employers sometimes welcome the idea of having first-rate talent available to them on an as-needed basis, rather than as a full-time employee. The challenge for the job seeker is one of communication. The resume and cover letter can be crafted to convey both solid competencies and a rational desire to work a nontraditional schedule.

RECOMMENDED APPROACH

As a nontraditional worker you have to make your availability known as a practicing professional whose only difference is situational—fully qualified, but not wanting to work full time. There are advantages to the employer as well as the worker in such arrangements. All that is needed is a meeting of the minds and that begins with a proper presentation of your credentials. Here are a few examples of traditional thinking that you should be prepared to cope with:

Possible Concern	Your Response
How could less than a full-time person possibly plan the annual meeting?	The job is a series of tasks to be accomplished, not hours to be logged. Let's discuss what has to be done and I'll show you how it can be done.

(cont'd)

Possible Concern	Your Response
You won't be able to get a feel for the working of our organization if you are only here part time.	Involvement and perceptiveness are not measured by hours in the presence of others. Has my reading of your requirements thus far been accurate?
How will we handle the question of taxes and benefits?	There are several approaches to that problem. If you want me to be an employee, then pay the taxes and provide partial benefits. If you prefer that I work as an independent contractor, a more arms-length relationship can be arranged.

These are just representative issues that might arise. If you have a particular orientation or want to steer the hiring in a certain direction, then things like the independent contractor vs. the part-time employee arrangements can be a part of your resume or cover letter.

RESUME TIPS

The question of resume model is an open one for the nontraditional worker. Basic qualities of the different resume formats becomes important, depending on your situation. If the proposed position flows logically from positions previously held, then the Work History Resume may be appropriate. Competency Cluster and Focused Resumes will be better if you are selling the ability to perform certain tasks without regard to length of time or settings in which you have been doing them.

A well-phrased OVERVIEW is the starting point for stating your case, with the understanding that the body of the resume will substantiate what you propose. An example of how that might be done follows:

> OVERVIEW: Paralegal with 6 year experience in the preparation of corporate documents seeks part-time employment in that specialty. Prefer to operate as an independent contractor accomplishing the work in my own office. Professionalism and respect for confidentiality verifiable by prominent local references.

This is a case where the desired situation has ben described, the terms under which the work would be accomplished stated, and an expected question answered. The groundwork has been laid for stating educational qualifications, specific abilities and achievements, and, possibly, concluding COMMENTS, such as:

> COMMENTS: Following 6 years of successful full-time employment in law firms, I am continuing my professional pursuits privately to insure the flexibility desired in the raising of my children.

The COMMENTS section is optional and would be used if there are points of clarification that might improve the reader's perception of what you are trying to accomplish.

Coming From Other Countries and Cultures

The United States is still a melting pot rich in the contributions and special talents of people coming here from other countries. The challenge for these job-seekers is in translating their experiences into terms that can be readily understood by U.S. employers. This can be done with a resume and cover letter especially designed for this purpose.

RECOMMENDED APPROACH

If you fit into the category, you must begin your job search with a candid evaluation of what you have to offer. You probably have educational and work experiences that will be valued by American employers. Enlist the assistance of an American friend to help you. See if you can translate your skills and capabilities into those valued by employers in this economy.

Once your competencies have been identified, you can begin the job search. Determine where your talents can be applied and the employers who could use your skills. Decide where you are willing to relocate in order to accept a position. Speak to people and organizations who might be of assistance. Locate publications that can alert you to the firms that might employ you. Read about them and watch for positions advertised. Draft a resume and cover letter that will carry your message to potential employers.

RESUME TIPS

If your past field of employment has a direct crossover into an American position, use the Work History Resume in the job search. However, the resume formats that will probably help you best in your new workplace are the Competency Cluster and Focused Resumes.

Chapter 1 includes a resume prepared by a Chinese student seeking professional employment in this country. Refer again to the resume of Lan Wang and the point-by-point explanations of how her case was made more convincing by altering the style and content of her resume. Here are some concerns common to foreign workers seeking employment in the United States and suggestions on how to cope.

Concern	Possible Solution
From my resume, the employer may not know how to address me—gender may not be apparent.	If such things are of concern, put Mr. or Ms. before your name or include a reference to gender in the OVERVIEW or elsewhere in your resume.
My schooling was not in a system equivalent to American schools and colleges.	Do your best to sort your educational experiences into categories that do equate to American levels—high school, junior college, trade school, or college. If a sentence of explanation would make it clearer, use it.

(cont'd)

Concern	Possible Solution
I will need my employer's support with visa considerations—how do I treat that subject?	Be honest about your immigration status, but do not make an issue of it. Objectively state the category that you hold and that to which you aspire—other details can be discussed later in the hiring process.
I want to establish that I can function in the American culture, that I understand the language and customs.	Demonstrate what you have done—earned a degree attending an American college, held a job that clearly required English language proficiency, etc.

In the final analysis, foreign students or workers face the same problem as other job candidates—making the point as directly and convincingly as possible that they know what the job entails and that they can do it. Writing a great resume and cover letter is one way to demonstrate both.

7 TRENDS IN THE WORK FORCE

"Most of the new jobs expected by 2000 will be in service-producing industries, especially retail trade, health services, and business services," according to Valerie A. Personick in an article for the *Monthly Labor Review* of the U. S. Department of Labor (1989). Manufacturing, farm, and traditional manual-labor occupations are not where the action is going to be in the coming decade.

Resumes play an increasingly important role as a larger percentage of the labor force competes for positions where the employer wants to know what you bring to the job in terms of training and work-related experience. More and more jobs require prospective employees to organize their thoughts and express them on paper—the job resume is an early test of that ability.

This chapter contains two tables designed to provide an easy review of the most dynamic employment categories for the 1990s. There are two ways to view these basic employment trends:

- the jobs categories with the *fastest rate of growth*; and
- the job categories with the *largest number of new jobs*.

Some fields will experience dramatic rates of growth, but still account for relatively few actual jobs. Other categories will lead the way in the actual number of new jobs created. The first table, **Fastest-Growing Occupations, 1988–2000**, is the place to look if you want to know what the fastest-growing fields of the 1990s are expected to be. If you want to temper the rate of growth with the reality of how many positions will be there to fill, look to the second table, **Occupations With Largest Job Growth, 1988–2000**. Between the two, you can identify where the greatest opportunities lie. (Both tables have been adapted from the projections of George Silvestri and John Lukasiewicz in their article, "Projections of Occupational Employment, 1989–2000," in the 1989 *Monthly Labor Review*.)

Fastest-Growing Occupations, 1988–2000[a]

Occupation	Number by 2000	Percent Change 1988–2000
Paralegals	145,000	75.3
Medical assistants	253,000	70.0
Home health aides	397,000	67.9
Radiologic technologists and technicians	218,000	66.0
Data-processing equipment repairers	115,000	61.2
Medical records technicians	75,000	59.9
Medical secretaries	327,000	58.0
Physical therapists	107,000	57.0
Surgical technologists	55,000	56.4
Operations research analysts	85,000	55.4
Securities and financial services sales workers	309,000	54.8
Travel agents	219,000	54.1
Computer systems analysts	617,000	53.3
Physical and corrective therapy assistants	60,000	52.5
Social welfare service aides	138,000	51.5
Occupational therapists	48,000	48.8
Computer programmers	769,000	48.1
Human services workers	171,000	44.9
Respiratory therapists	79,000	41.3
Correction officers and jailers	262,000	40.8

[a] Adapted from Silvestri & Lukasiewicz (1989), Table 5, page 60.

Occupations With Largest Job Growth, 1988–2000[a]

Occupation	Number by 2000	Percent Change 1988–2000
Salespersons, retail	4,564,000	19.0
Registered nurses	2,190,000	38.8
Janitors and cleaners, including maids and housekeeping cleaners	3,450,000	19.2
Waiters and waitresses	2,337,000	30.9

(cont'd)

Occupation	Number by 2000	Percent Change 1988–2000
General managers and top executives	3,509,000	15.8
General office clerks	2,974,000	18.1
Secretaries, except legal and medical	3,288,000	13.2
Nursing aides, orderlies, and attendants	1,562,000	31.9
Truck drivers, light and heavy	2,768,000	15.4
Receptionists and information clerks	1,164,000	39.8
Cashiers	2,614,000	13.2
Guards	1,050,000	32.2
Computer programmers	769,000	48.1
Food counter, fountain, and related workers	1,866,000	14.7
Food preparation workers	1,260,000	22.8
Licensed practical nurses	855,000	36.6
Teachers, secondary school	1,388,000	19.2
Computer systems analysts	617,000	53.3
Accountants and auditors	1,174,000	22.0
Teachers, kindergarten and elementary	1,567,000	15.3

[a] Adapted from Silvestri & Lukasiewicz (1989), Table 6, page 60.

What does all of this mean to you as an employee casting your well-prepared resume in a sea of likely employers? In their book *Jobs! What They Are . . . Where They Are . . . What They Pay!*, Anne and Robert Snelling have this advice:

> While two equally talented beginners may eventually reach comparable levels of career success, the job seeker who starts out in a promising field is almost surely destined to move farther faster than the one who aspires to work in a field that is experiencing little or no growth. Being aware of today's trends is one sure way of choosing a field that is destined to grow. [p. 23]

So whether you are a beginner at the entry-level stage or an early retiree starting a second career, examine the trends that your government makes so readily available. If you are have the choice, steer your career in the direction of growth where the opportunities will best accommodate your ambitions and abilities.

Michael Kiernan, writing in *U.S. News & World Report* (September 25, 1989) took a broad view of the trends for the 1990s that will affect prospective job seekers. In addition to being aware of growing employment fields for the decade, he stressed the necessity of being prepared for them with the necessary skills.

> Better educated workers who can adapt to new technologies will discover many new jobs awaiting them in the next decade. Poorly educated workers

unwilling or unable to learn new skills will find little that will pay enough to support a family. More than a gap between the rich and the poor, say the experts, the dividing line for working America in the 1990s will be between those who have learned how to learn and those who have not. [p. 62]

The adaptability that Kiernan emphasized relates directly to the skillful use of a resume in articulating your education and abilities to a constantly evolving job market. A simple chronology, lacking at least some attention to focusing your talents on the position in question, may place you at a disadvantage. As American work life becomes more a series of adaptations to changing opportunities, and less a cradle-to-grave endurance march, expect to become an advocate of your cumulative worth to the next employer. Your resume will be the vehicle for accomplishing that goal—both in your own mind (through planning and preparing) and in the eyes of those evaluating you for a situation that may be quite different from the one you are leaving (by reading a resume that is structured to communicate why you are the person for the job).

The next few years promise to be a challenging and—for those with the ability to work the system—a rewarding time. Displaying your carefully presented education and experience will call for resume-writing abilities that do those talents justice in the exciting and lucrative job market that is materializing.

BIBLIOGRAPHY

Bolles, Richard N. *What Color Is Your Parachute?* Berkeley: Ten Speed Press, 1990.

Carey, John. "The Changing Face of a Restless Nation." *Business Week*, Number 3125, 92–106 (September 25, 1989).

Davis, Richard S. "Have You Tried a Notice of Availability?" *Adult and Continuing Education*, XIX (17), 7 (September 11, 1989).

Jackson, Tom. *The Perfect Resume.* New York: Anchor/Doubleday, 1981.

Johnston, William B. and Packer, Arnold H. *Workforce 2000: Work and Workers for the 21st Century.* Washington: U. S. Department of Labor, June 1987.

Kiernan, Michael; Moore, Lisa J.; and Silver, Marc. "Best Jobs for the Future: The Message for the Next Decade Is to Retrain and Retrain." *U. S. News & World Report*, 107 (12), 60–71 (September 25, 1989).

Kiplinger, Austin H. and Kiplinger, Knight A. *America in the Global '90s*, Washington: Kiplinger Books, 1989.

Occupational Outlook Handbook, 1988–89 Edition. U. S. Department of Labor, Lincolnwood, IL: VGM Career Horizons, 1988.

Opportunity 2000. Washington: U. S. Department of Labor, September 1988.

Owens, Peta. "Hire Away." *New Business Opportunities*, 1 (5), 60–65 (September 1989).

Personick, Valeria A. "Industry Output and Employment: A Slower Trend for the Nineties." U. S. Department of Labor: *Monthly Labor Review*, 112 (11), 25 (November 1989).

Reed, Jean, editor. *Resumes That Get Jobs.* New York: ARCO/Simon & Schuster, 1986.

Richardson, Douglas B. "The Confessions of a Skeptical Resume Reader: What Happens When Your Resume is 1 of 400." Dow Jones: *National Business Employment Weekly* reprint (undated).

Rottman, David. "How to Get Interviews Using Market Letters: A New, More Efficient Approach to Reaching Decision-Makers." Dow Jones: *National Business Employment Weekly* reprint (undated).

Ryckman, W. G. "Seasoned Executives Emphasize Accomplishments: Alter Format of Resumes, Cover Letters." Dow Jones: *National Business Employment Weekly* reprint (undated).

Schuman, Nancy and Lewis, William. *Revising Your Resume*. New York: John Wiley & Sons, 1987.

Schwartz, Lester and Brechner, Irv. *The Career Finder, Pathways to Over 1500 Entry-Level Jobs*. New York: Ballantine Books/Random House, 1982.

Silvestri, George and Lukasiewicz, John. "Projections of Occupational Employment, 1988–2000." U. S. Department of Labor: *Monthly Labor Review*, 112 (11), 42–65 (November 1989).

Snelling, Robert O. and Snelling, Anne M. *Jobs! What They Are . . . Where They Are . . . What They Pay! The Seven Top Entry-Level Job Areas*. New York: Fireside/Simon & Schuster, 1989.

Washington, Tom. "Creating a Resume With Qualifications: Add Summary Statement for Emphasis." Dow Jones: *National Business Employment Weekly* reprint (undated).

NOTES

NOTES

NOTES

NOTES

NOTES

NOTES

NOTES

NOTES

NOTES

NOTES